Peter was born in Flaxton (north of York) the third of four children. He attended Maltby Grammar School and after a failed attempt to join the R.A.F. (sent home for being underage), he enlisted in the Royal Navy, was demobbed in 1946 and consequently retired from British Steel as head of the Works Study department in Parkgate.

He then filled his time with painting, fishing, mind puzzles and the writing of these memoirs.

Dedication

This book is dedicated to my wife Iris:
She always wondered what I got up to during the war since I
had rarely talked about it.
Some of the answers are here.

P.R. Ellis

An Experience of War 1939/1945

AUSTIN MACAULEY PUBLISHERS™

LONDON • CAMBRIDGE • NEW YORK • SHARJAH

A CIP catalogue record for this title is available from the British Library.

ISBN 9781786295187 (Paperback)
ISBN 9781786295194 (Hardback)
ISBN 9781786295200 (E-Book)
www.austinmacauley.com

First Published (2017)
Austin Macauley Publishers Ltd.
25 Canada Square
Canary Wharf
London
E14 5LB

Acknowledgements

June and Tony Bird: without whose initial encouragement and invaluable help in typing the first draft, the book would never have been out of the handwritten stage. Stuart and Christopher Ellis who overcame a myriad of problems to transpose it into a workable document on my computer.

Lynne Smith (Nee Ellis): who kept reminding me that our Grandchildren also wanted to know what I did during the war and what it was like. She also encouraged me to talk to the junior school children at Hasland on the subject for several years.

Gail and Colin: who gave freely of their time and undertook the daunting task of proofreading. Aimee, Ellen and Gavin, who kept reminding me they hadn't yet got a copy!

Jimmy Brown, author of "Harry Tate's Navy": whose research I have shamelessly used in the early stages of this book. I hope he will forgive me. All the people whose names I never knew and who helped from the end of a telephone with the research, sometimes just by pointing me in the right direction by clarifying a situation.

ROYE (Peter)

The silver badge exclusive to men of the Royal Naval Patrol service with at least six months' service at sea.

Combined Operations

These few memories are based on my wartime experience and thus not strictly an Autobiography, but not to worry, all autobiographies are selective! Their main purpose is to tell the whole truth. About other people!

If you take a chance in life, sometimes good things happen, sometimes bad things happen;

If you don't take a chance,

Nothing happens!

Prologue

"The past is a foreign land, they do things differently there!"

This account of one very ordinary experience of the 1939/45 War was written, I suppose, as a result of my vanity. In the early years, after the war had finished, I had no inclination to talk about it to anyone. Not due to the experiences that had so shocked the mind as to make it a "no go" area, so much as a rude awakening from idealistic youth to the realities of the lengths to which "humanity" was capable of going in pursuance of their own beliefs. I went into the war with ideas which had been fuelled by First World War pilots who, of course, told only of the thrill of catching an opponent on the wrong end of the guns and surviving against incredible odds a "war to end all wars!"

Stories of boy sailors winning Victoria Crosses at Jutland, and the unimaginable courage of one-legged soldiers who had lived through the trench warfare, conducted, supported and encouraged by what we now know as the "Donkey Generals" who, on both sides, were lionized by people who should, and most likely did, know better. In short, I came to the conclusion that the least said about it the better, and perhaps my children would not grow up with the same mistaken ideals that I had developed.

However, as the years passed, and as a result of seeing the changes being implemented by people, who for the most part, had never put their lives at risk for any reason whatsoever and certainly not for their fellow men, I began to feel a new respect for the "idiots" like myself, who had fought, rightly or wrongly for what we thought was freedom, independence and the right to decide for ourselves. Just goes to show, one cannot be right all the time! Anyway, instead of letting my son play with my campaign medals as toys, I gradually came to treasure them as a symbol of an age forever gone, and as a result re-ribboned and polished them. Having, as I have said, never told anyone (including my wife) of just what I did in the war, I began to come under some pressure to describe it. Since each Armistice Day I was unashamedly proud to put on my medals, this is hardly surprising.

Over the years, with grandchildren to consider, as well as wife and children, I have finally decided to write it down and let others judge it if they feel so inclined, or simply accept it as an account of one of the influences that shaped my temperament. As has occasionally been pointed out to me, there must be some reason for it!!

If you want to read further, on your own head be it!

"Each man's death diminishes me for I am a part of mankind. Therefore seek not to know for whom the Bell tolls; it tolls for thee!"

Note. Since these memoirs were not written until 1990, some forty-five plus years after the events, there may well be errors of chronological sequence or events clearly remembered but wrongly ascribed to particular occasions. In addition, much research was necessary to provide relevant detail, and it is not pretended that memory has provided the only source.

Some periods, during war service, have disappeared from memory altogether. For example, when I left Malta to take a commission, I boarded H.M.S. Mauritius, a cruiser. From that moment, which I remember distinctly, I have no idea how I reached Greenock until I again saw a railway coal wagon marked MALTBY. I know that my arrival in Greenock was on a troopship and not on Mauritius, but I cannot recall the name. There may well be other occasions, but none so clearly defined.

I choose to write in narrative form rather than simply note dates, places, times and events in the hope that it will be easier and perhaps, more interesting for a reader.

As I have pointed out before I could be wrong!

One more thing: I know nothing of the laws of libel and I have not sought permission to mention the events described. In consequence, all names have been changed with the exception of those in the public domain from records accessible to everyone. This does, of course, include the names of the party and other units mentioned.

The Royal Naval Patrol Service, 'Harry Tate's Navy' as it was popularly known, was a very special service with its own rules and regulations and the unique distinction of having its own exclusive silver badge, worn by sea going officers and ratings alike.

Its headquarters were at the Sparrow's Nest, the municipal pleasure ground at Lowestoft, and its fighting fleet consisted of requisitioned trawlers, whalers, drifters, paddle steamers, yachts, tugs and sundry other vessels. 'Minor War Vessels' they were called by the Admiralty.

Armed with out-of-date weapons, they set out, not only from Lowestoft, but also from many other small ports to fight the War in any corner of the globe they could be of use. Moreover, R.N.P.S. ratings served with Combined Operations Units on operations I have not been able to find any official recognition of.

The museum at Sparrow's Nest in Lowestoft has many exhibits, which receive scant recognition outside the Veteran's Association and few realize that 2,385 shipmates lost their lives and have no grave but the sea.

Jimmy Brown, author of 'Harry Tate's Navy', has blazed the trail to awareness of a little known, but nonetheless extremely important and undoubtedly courageous, service through two World Wars.

What follows is another single story of the same service. As Jimmy says, it cannot attempt to be a complete account because no one man will ever know the whole story of 'Harry Tate's Navy'!

The story starts not in 1939 as might have been imagined. Not even in 1914! Back in 1907, Admiral Lord Charles Beresford, who, at that time, commanded the Channel Fleet, suggested that the Admiralty should purchase a number of fishing trawlers for use as experimental minesweepers. The Admiralty, apparently, looked favourably on the suggestion and in 1910 a Trawler section of the Royal Naval Reserve was created with the new rank of Skipper RNR instituted as the most appropriate for its officers. Equivalent to the then Warrant Officer in the Royal Navy, entry was open to fishing skippers between the ages of twenty-five and forty-five who possessed a Board of Trade Certificate of Competency and who had held command for two years or more. They served for five years at a time up to twenty years and received an annual retainer and full pay when called up for service or training. Entry to the lower deck was open to experienced fishermen as Second Hand, Engineman, Deckhand and Trimmer on the same terms up to a total of twenty-five years. All ranks received a course on minesweeping.

At the start of the First World War in 1914, the Admiralty requisitioned 150 trawlers for minesweeping but before the war was many weeks old, it was obvious that this was totally inadequate. The Germans were laying mines, not only around the Moray Firth, the Grand Fleet's main anchorage, but in every seaway around the world which could be used by British shipping. This, with total disregard for non-belligerent and neutral cargo or passenger transports.

Minesweeping was therefore, a global operation and when the Armistice was signed in 1918 the RNR trawler section had expanded from 1,200 officers and men to 39,000. After the war ended the minesweepers took another 12 months to clear both the enemy and allied mines.

In 1919, when this task was finished, the trawler section of the RNR was reformed as the RNR Patrol Service. Since in addition to their minesweeping, many vessels had been employed on a variety of different duties, ranging from harbour defence to convoy protection and escort. In line with traditional political expediency and blindness the number of vessels and manpower was pared and diminished in the 'tween war year until only a handful of trawlers were retained under the white ensign. These were based on H.M.S. Boscawen at Portland and it was there that new entrants to the RNR Patrol Service went for their biennial training. Portland also housed the training establishment for the then-new anti-submarine device – ASDIC,[1] at H.M.S. Osprey.

In the 1939-1945 War, the R.N.P.S. personnel took on not only minesweeping, convoy escort and protection and coastal defence, but also included combined operation activities in their versatile repertoire. Some people still believe the regular armed forces won the war! They didn't! Without the 'wet behind the ears' HO's, they were never in with a chance. What they did do was provide the backbone of skill, courage and experience which welded the lot into an invincible whole. As Hitler found to his cost!

The shilling-sized silver emblem worn on the left forearm is unique to the Patrol Service. It was initiated by Winston Churchill and took the form of a shield with a sinking shark transfixed by a marline spike to symbolise the A/S[2] service against a background of fishing nets in which mines were trapped representing the M/S[3]. The shield was surrounded by a rope with two fisherman's bend knots topped by a naval crown with a scroll beneath bearing the letters "M/S ~ A/ S".

The badge, worn by both officers and ratings, was only awarded for six months service afloat on either of the two branches with a few exceptions that merited special consideration. My own was one such case and resulted

---

1 ASDIC was an early form of echo sounder and the initials were of Allied Submarine Detection Investigation Committee.

2 Anti-submarine

3 Mine-sweepers

from the activities with the M.F.V. in mine clearance and
booby-trap dismantling in Ostende.

'Thou'lt find thy manhood all too fast –
Soon come, soon gone, and age at last,
A sorry breaking-up'
From an Ode by Thomas Hood

1942

The War had been going on since September 1939 and it was now September 1942. Little else had any significance to a 17 year old, and I had left Grammar School in the belief that I could join the fighting forces immediately. Wrong! I had to find a job, which I did with a Borough Police Force as a cadet telephone operator. At this time (Sept. '42), I volunteered for the R.A.F. At 17 years old and knowing nothing but war for three years, I was stupid enough to think war was somehow glamorous and romantic! With that attitude, I was getting concerned that we might run out of war before I got to have a go! I suppose that was constant propaganda, and a diet of too much Morte d'Arthur and Rupert Brooke, and not enough Wilfred Owen and the realistic poets, to say nothing of the exploits of Bulldog Drummond and Biggles!

Be that as it may, and my education was definitely Arts biased, I found myself entrained for Darlington, courtesy of an R.A.F. rail warrant, in short order.

For one who had never been further than Cleethorpes with the family, it was quite an experience. First hurdle was a physical examination, and since I had virtually lived in the woods as a boy and frequently climbed 70 ft. trees, the outcome was never in doubt. Next came five days of concentrated academic tests; English, Maths, Physics, Geography and General Knowledge and aptitude biased to all things R.A.F. None of it was any problem I was accepted for pilot training and offered Fighters, with the unspoken indication that to choose anything else would not be looked on kindly. With hindsight, we had been losing rather a lot at that time (Fighter Pilots that is).

My training had started immediately on my acceptance and included 'flying' a Miles Magister, with the Pilot behind doing the taking off and landing. The purpose of this was to find out right at the start if flying affected me adversely as it does many people. It was a long time afterwards that I learned that this flight, had I remained in the R.A.F., would have been the only time I was allowed in a plane for many months.

On the seventh day of my training, disaster struck! It was discovered, and I never found out how, that I was not yet eighteen, and I was sent home immediately. The reason I lasted seven days was that I had blurred everything in the DOB sections on all relevant forms.

Being severely put out by this treatment, I immediately volunteered for the Navy. They accepted me, knowing my correct age, but still out-flanked me by not sending for me until after I was eighteen in December of that year. In fact I was called before Christmas, but was not to report until 4/1/43.

Another rail warrant, this time courtesy of the Royal Navy, and down to Portsmouth. I was met at the station by a Navy shore patrol, all belts and gaiters, and my introduction to the fact that in initial Navy training, all orders, instructions, requests or casual conversation were conducted at the loudest possible shout. Bundled into a canvas topped 5 tonner, and driven to Fareham and H.M.S. Collingwood, as though our arrival was a matter of dire emergency, it was certainly a matter of incredible luck! Having been allocated to Foretop division (whatever that meant!), I gratefully turned in at 11.30 p.m. along with a hut full of other new entries. No sooner had I shut my eyes than bugles blasted out Reveille, and a dapper C.P.O. – C.P.O. Cook – a West Country man with a DCM and Bar amongst all his campaign ribbons from both wars I discovered later, again in immaculate belt and gaiters (at 5.30 am!) rousted everybody to fall in on the parade ground. With much shouting and bawling, we eventually discovered what this 'falling in' meant, but not before two unfortunates amongst us learned also that one did not walk on the parade ground. (I did have some slight advantage with parade ground etiquette since I had risen to the rank of Staff Sergeant in the Army cadets at home. You will, no doubt, have noticed by this time, that I have been a soldier, airman and now a sailor, at least in name.) One doubled (this meant ran). The acquisition of this knowledge cost them three days' kitchen duties, and the rest of us the sudden awareness that one should never be in the wrong place at the wrong time. All this before we even had a uniform.

Uniforms were issued and any minor misfits were to be corrected – we were issued with 'housewives' needles (2), cotton (blue), cotton (white) and scissors (small), all in a roll-up canvas – before the next parade. This done, another medical, various jabs, in case we might need them and some doubling round the parade ground just to get us used to the idea. One end of the parade ground held a 100 ft. mast with cross members and rigging in the form of netting. (You may have seen it used at Earls Court on television.) We climbed this regularly every week and each week the time allowed was reduced. Without any boasting, I was rarely beaten at this since climbing either trees or ropes had been one of my boyhood pleasures. On top of the mast the capping disc (referred to as the button) was about 15 inches in diameter. Each week, one trainee was selected for the honour (?) of the button (his only support was in fact a six foot length of rope round his waist and secured just below the button). I might add that I was not too unhappy when I failed to be selected for this honour.

Despite the emphasis on physical fitness which was reinforced by all manner of means, like 10 mile runs in full gear, assault courses through all manner of obstacles and daily workouts with the P.T.I. (Physical Training Instructors) – sadistic beasts imported from Nazi Germany we all believed at the time – we were also mentally battered with things like Morse Code, semaphore, navigation, searnanship and boat handling, to say nothing of King's Rules and Admiralty Instructions (K.R.'s and A.I.'s). These latter were the indisputable Bible of the Navy. One may, and many did, blaspheme as much as the inclination took one, with quite remarkable impunity, but should one break one of the K.R's and A.I's then eternal damnation and hellfire would have been a welcome relief. Having survived one of these action-filled days until 7:00 p.m., an early night to recover sufficiently to face the morning was the height of my ambition. Poor misguided youth! No sooner had we been fed, (not before we had been showered – dirty flesh was a heinous crime in the 'Andrew'),[4] we would seek to clean our uniforms and boots to face the minutely detailed morning inspection before another soul – destroying day started. Failure meant that what free time we might salvage from a normal day would be filled to overflowing with K.P. duties, which usually consisted of a 'midnight high' pile of potatoes to be peeled. But…. and I do mean but, our venerable and much loved divisional C.P.O. was in competition with all the other C.P.O's and jaunties and crushers, as to who had the best intake of recruits, particularly in respect of boxing! Neither metric nor imperial weight values were of any consequence in this situation. Nor were any personal views on the noble art of pugilism or fisticuffs, or self-defence or however else one cared to describe it. When "Chiefie" wandered down the centre of our immaculate (God help us if it wasn't) barrack room, he simply looked at what he considered a reasonable size and said, "At 9 p.m. you will fall in, in gym kit in the main NAAFI hall where you will be fighting for the honour of the Foretop Division at Flyweight, Bantamweight, Heavyweight, or whatever" – pause – "And I should add that my Division has not lost a decision in six months, and should you by some mischance bring disgrace (and a considerable loss of

---

[4] The origination of the Royal Navy being called "The Andrew" stems from the war against Napoleon. Naval ships were crewed by men impressed by the 'Press Gangs', the most successful of these was said to be under the leadership of one Andrew Miller. So many men were taken by him that the fleet was said to be "Andrew Miller's Navy", from that the term was shortened to the "Andrew"

income) to this part of the ship, then the halcyon existence you have all enjoyed so far will dissipate as the early morning mists which I might add, you will have every opportunity of observing at around 4:30 am. For the rest of your holiday here! Do I make myself clear?"

He did! I was chosen at Welterweight. I suppose I was around, give or take half a stone, nine stone at that time, but I wished I had hung back a bit on that blasted weekly mast climb. First over got you noticed! As it turned out there were two things in my favour. One, the lad I was fighting was not, perhaps, as well motivated as our psychologist (Chiefie) had made me, and two, Chiefie was the referee on that occasion! Suffice to say that by some strange coincidence, our other lads won too and dawn did not break until normal at 5:30 a.m.!

Those were wonderful days before anyone took a shot at us in anger, that is, if those live rounds a couple of inches above our heads when we were trying to cross rough ground unseen, were of a friendly nature!

In view of all the gunnery, we were being crammed with, .303 rifles, .45 automatics, 20mm Oerlikons, 40mm Bofors and 4.5" to name but a few, we were expected to participate, following the theory by spending a day at Whale Island and putting it into practice. Rifle training and bayonet practice was, of course, carried out on the range at the camp. Sorry, I should say H.M.S. Collingwood. An unfortunate incident occurred in as much as the gunnery officer assigned to my group had gone up the hill without his binoculars. The largest guns were at the bottom of the hill and the smallest at the top. We were firing Bofors from about midway at drogues, towed by aircraft. Before the shooting started I was dispatched to the gunnery control office at the hill bottom to fetch said binoculars. Returning, I was just clear of the 4.5" guns when the target was flown over. Everything on the hill opened fire and I was struck, not only by the noise, but also by the shock waves from displaced air. Ear plugs had been issued in my absence!

At that stage, being completely deaf and in some pain, I was returned to sick bay as soon as possible. Diagnosis was that hearing would return in a few days, and although some discharge may occur, no serious damage was done and to "Keep taking the tablets!" Would that I had known then what I know now! Hearing did return and life sped on to the end of training. We discovered that C.P.O. Cook was a veteran both of the 1914-18 War, and a survivor of two destroyers and Dunkirk in this one! He had trained us hard and well and given a bunch of naive civilian boys a sudden shock awareness of a real and unforgiving world that might just possibly enable us to survive whatever might befall us. Hated for three months, he was suddenly regarded with an affectionate respect.

A week's leave, in which I and I think, the others, strutted around proudly at home like real sailors. On return, our intake was posted immediately to Lowestoft, and instead of being P/JX 4****4 I became LT/JX 4****4. This meant that instead of being a Portsmouth (P) general service rating, I had now become a Lowestoft (LT) Royal Naval/Patrol Service rating. I didn't have much time to ponder the significance, if any, of this because after a much delayed, shunted and side-tracked rail journey, my arrival was greeted with an instruction to draw Arctic clothing, stow it in the appointed mess – draw a rail warrant and proceed on a 14-day embarkation leave.

The Barracks was called "The Sparrow's Nest" and had been a holiday camp (H.M.S. EUROPA was its official title). On return, there we were jabbed with everything we had not already had, and in a couple of days took another 48 hour train journey which disgorged us on the dockside at Greenock. The first thing I noticed was a railway Wagon with MALTBY in big white letters on it. That made me homesick before I had even set foot on the ship.

The troop carrier we boarded was SS BAMFORA I think, and once loaded we lay off in the Clyde estuary for five days before the convoy was eventually built up and set off for God knows where. We certainly did not! The old hands on the ship – and there weren't many – knowingly informed us that since we had been issued with Arctic clothing, we would undoubtedly be going to the Tropics. After a while, I thought they were not too far wrong. I did not know much about ships and the sea at that time, but I did know where the sun rose and set! For the duration of the passage I had been made part of the number 2 (standby) 4.5" gun crew on the stern. Number 1 gun crew had actually fired one! And were therefore spared much watch-keeping and only called to man the gun when Action Stations were sounded. This turned out to be very frequently because the Bay of Biscay had its fair share of the U-boats and long-range Condors trying to steer them in, U-boats that is. I only recall one being attacked, and the outcome was, to me, unknown.

That stern end slapped up and down with monotonous regularity and I was so seasick for four days and nights that I would never even have noticed, and far less cared, if we had gone down with all hands. As it turns out I have never been seasick since.

The Straits of Gibraltar marked the end of my misery, but I was nearly court-martialled for being asleep on the gun from utter exhaustion. Fortunately for me, the officer who caught me was more aware of my problems, and having lectured me about how the Italians had lost most of their fleet at Matapan due to sleeping watch keepers, sent me to get two more life jackets and told me to put them behind the ready-use lockers out of everyone's way, and to be damned sure to be bright-eyed and bushy-tailed when the Bridge Officers could see this far astern in the morning.

As it was, I lost the next hour in my fascination at St Elmo's fire playing round our mastheads as we were met by a tremendous electrical storm.

Algiers was our first port of call, on Good Friday. It looks superb from ten miles out: all white and pastel pinks and blues. From three miles it smelled like an open sewer, and alongside it was filthy, strewn with rubbish, and the harbour water was so foetid that one would have died of poisoning before drowning on the misfortune of falling in.

I Became shore based from the 'trooper', being transferred to H.M.S. Hannibal – 25/4/43 – again transferred to the control of H.M.S. Hamilcar. These were not ships, but merely administration units, although they had barrack quarters for Transients passing through.

I was Drafted aboard L.S.T. 424, American-built and welded not riveted, they would flex visibly in almost any weather. The Americans claimed they were perfect for the job for which they were designed since their shallow draft precluded them from being torpedoed. I later learned to my cost that this was not so! So did the unfortunate Americans on L.S.T. 239 in Lyme Bay off Slapton Sands in a rehearsal for Utah beach! *Landing Ship Tank* 424. This was the MK2 version – 300 ft. in length, opening bow doors with a ramp which could then be lowered, and a hoist from the lower tank-space to the upper deck. They drew 3'7" when loaded with 2000 tons, and 18 inches when sailing light. In consequence they could roll in a flat calm. We sailed in convoy again, heading east and although our destination, Bougie (now I believe called Bougea), was only about 100 miles down the coast, we were attacked by Stukas and JU88s coming in relays, apparently from Pantellaria. We had some near misses and my first real display of a concerted anti-aircraft umbrella barrage. Very noisy, but quite pretty in the hours of darkness. It was to lose any attraction it may have had on that score in the next few months! A tanker sailing between us and the shore, presumably to offer more protection from submarines, took a direct hit. There were no survivors, and the blaze was only dimmed by dawn and the sun rising, even though we were many miles away by that time.

Bougie was a small port; dusty and straggling but far cleaner than Algiers. I should mention that in Algiers we had been organised from the original 100 leaving Lowestoft, into groups of 20 with one officer and one PO or leading seaman. These were not necessarily R.N.P.S. Each group was named, I think, after parts of the anchor system – shackle, fluke, ring, etc. Ours was called Party Cable and was commanded by a Commissioned Warrant Officer named Ashwood and a leading seaman called Whitemore.

Both men were much older than we 'sprogs' but we were to find out later that we could not have been in better hands. In 1992 I have learned that there were seven groups and all were called Party Cable. The names of the officers commanding each group were:

Ashwood (Harry) D.S.C. later

Davison

Rendall

Lucas

Siddons

Johnson

There were several Londoners in our group but the only one I took to was Joe Newell. Joe was a few years older than me and wiser in naval lore. I learned later he had already got 3 years' service in: a good friend to have. The issue of Combined Operation shoulder flashes and the Khaki battle dress brought with it the information that we had been attached to a Commando, and following a crash course at Djidjelli on unarmed combat, survival, and simple explosives, we would henceforth be considered 'Commandos'. The knife that all commandos were issued with had been designed by a policeman, and was normally worn in a scabbard sewn to the trouser leg or boots; his name was Fairchild. What we were issued with was a 'baby Fairchild'. It was smaller than the standard one and was worn strapped to the forearm, between wrists and the bend in the elbow, butt to the wrist end. (Mine disappeared in the blank period after boarding 'Mauritius'.) No polite enquiry about whether we would like to volunteer, just a "get fell in three deep and get on with it."

Returned to Bougie bruised, battered and very tired. The following morning we were told that after our 'Holiday' we now had some work to do, and were asked which of us could drive? I couldn't, but I broke a golden rule and volunteered anyway. What I was required to drive was a RUSTON BUCYRUS mobile crane (wheels – not track).

Having had at least 3 or 4 car rides before joining up, I thought there couldn't be too much to it!

A sapper from the R.E.'s demonstrated how it worked and left me to it. I got it going and managed to drive right through the town to where there was enough desert to turn round (he hadn't shown me how to reverse!) and came all the way back again. Piece of cake. I expected instant approval and next instruction. I got the latter, rapidly and succinctly. I had left the jib raised and taken out the complete telephone system leaving Bougie cut off from all except radio communications.

The Town Marshall and Army Major named, if my memory serves, McNeil was – I'm told – quite pleased at temporary relief from the bombardment of orders from Algiers, Bone and Tripoli. Nevertheless he made enquiries about which side I was on, and promised to come to the docks and shoot me another day when it was more convenient! Each of our groups was required to assemble steel causeways. Ours not to reason why! They were built in two sections 140ft long and roughly 5 ft. wide, from steel boxes 7x5x5 feet, fastened together by angle irons along four edges.

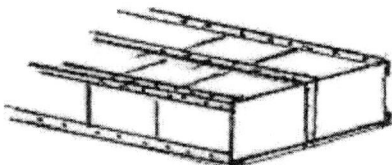

The purpose of these was still unknown to us. They had been designed by Captain John N. Haycock of the U.S. Navy, and we learned they were to be used in relatively shallow water to land both men and vehicles swiftly where the landing craft could not get right on to the beach, and perhaps more importantly off again.

We tested them for many weeks up and down the North African coast, in all sorts of conditions, both day and night. The basic idea was to tie one each side of the L.S.T., run for the beach (with us on the pontoons), slip them and go full astern. The pontoon crews then had to bring them together and anchor them on the beach.

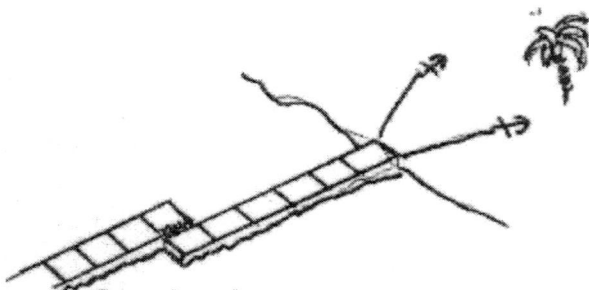

There was no engine just one big stern oar for steering, and a big box of nuts and bolts and tools for linking up the two sections. The amazing thing was 80% of the time it worked! On one occasion, we found the skeleton of an old World War One plane (French), on another we played Rugby whilst the L.S.T. ran down the coast. The most memorable event was when the tow on my pontoon parted in rough seas. For six hours we were completely adrift with no water, no food, no land, and no ship under a blazing sun.

With only 12" above water, we could see virtually no distance, and remaining on that flat platform in a 10ft sea was not easy. L.S.T.424 eventually found us again, but we learned afterwards that they had passed within half a mile on two sweeps without seeing us! Made me realise what the odds were for ditched airmen against being recovered!

With the practising over, we moved down the coast, to Philippeville I think, to load troops and vehicles. Having a reputation as a driver! I was included in a party being driven 10 miles into the desert to a R.E.M.E. workshop. We were to collect vehicles recovered from the desert and renovated, and bring them back to port for use in the next stage of the war. I got a balloon-tyred ambulance which wouldn't go very fast When it caught fire, I found out why. I had forgotten to take off the handbrake! I got the fire out alright and delivered it to the docks.

Next trip I was allocated to a 10 ton MACK with trailer. At least 8 forward gears and two reverse. Having got it to the docks on 3 of those I found, when I was broadside on to the ramp, that reversing with a trailer was not in my repertoire. I slipped out of the opposite door when MP's came to find out why it was blocking all loading.

Between the practising and loading, we had done two runs with supplies further east, presumably for the Eighth Army.

These were night drops and though we encountered no opposition from air, sea, or land, we were (to our surprise) eligible for the African Star and entitled to wear the numeral 8 on the ribbon. Needless to say, it was not issued to us at that time.

Once the vehicles were loaded on, we sailed down the coast to Sousse and embarked troops. We had Senegalese under French Officers, Americans and British troops. On passage now and the destination was unknown, but the pontoons were lashed alongside. As it turned out it was little short of a miracle that they arrived at our eventual landfall with us.

On board we had the famous Stooges of film fame to entertain the troops. Most films only feature three of them, but my memory says four: Larry, Shemp, Moe and Curly. In the evenings when not called on to man the gun or take a watch as lookout, or Bosun's Mate (Dogsbody), I watched them playing Poker and very skilful they were too. They invited me to play, which I did, but not for money because we were not paid during that period, except for a small amount of Military currency to spend in the ship's canteen. Having beaten me on every hand, despite the high quality of hands I was dealt, they then showed me how it was possible to manipulate the cards.

The tricks that they used were, they said, learned in Las Vegas and Reno. Wherever they were learned they were highly effective and I found them impossible to spot. During this evening many gags were pulled, and at one point I pulled my forelock over my eye, put a black comb end across my upper lip, frowned and rattled off some gibberish German in my schooldays impression of Hitler. The Stooges, immediately invited me to repeat it in their sketch on the upper deck the following day. They wrote a little bit of dialogue into what they had already arranged, and we used the hoist from tank space to upper deck as a rising stage. Everyone enjoyed their clowning around including me, but at the end of an hour the sea was

34

beginning to shorten and the wind was piping up. I think I might have mentioned before that an L.S.T. with practically no keel was not the most comfortable ship to be on when the weather started to get rough. That was something of an understatement. Mountainous waves as high as a seven storey building with the wind whipping the white crests into mist lifted us towards the clouds. A nerve-shattering pause and then we were hurled down like a lift with a broken cable. Bows disappeared in angry foam and the shock almost loosened teeth at the bottom.

These all-welded ships were prone to a whipping action in heavy seas which increased the risk of them breaking their backs. In fact the last two days of the cruise brought some of the worst storms I have ever sailed in, including Biscay! A Polish-manned L.S.T. was lost with all hands when it turned turtle. What sleep I could snatch was taken in the thwartship passage at deck level, sliding from one side to the other. Used life jackets were used to cushion the bulkheads at the end of each slide. That, I believe, was the start of my claustrophobia.

We were briefed on what we were required to do several hours before D-day. (Yes, it was always known as D-day long before the Normandy Landings.) Destination was Sicily. Operation "Husky". History's largest invasion fleet, numbering 3300 ships. Seven divisions in the Assault wave, which is two more than those landings in Normandy a year later. I make no excuse for making the point once again that the Allied invasion of Sicily was the biggest amphibious operation ever planned. If the landings in Sicily and Italy had failed, and the later ones came close to it, there would have been no Normandy beach-heads on the 6th June 1944.

Command of this task force was given to Vice Admiral Sir Bertram Ramsay, who answered to Britain's greatest ever (in my view) admiral, Admiral A.B. Cunningham.

The landings were timed for 6:30am on the Cent beach, and 3:30am on How beach on the morning of July 10th 1943.

Americans were to take Joss, Dime and Cent beaches south west of Pachino Peninsular, and the British beaches were Bark West, Bark South, Bark East, Acid South and Acid North, stretching to just south of Syracuse. Acid north was split into HOW and AMBER.

The convoy had, of course, been spotted by Condor reconnaissance planes. With 3,300 ships, there was no way it could have been missed, but despite this few air attacks had been mounted by the Germans, and none at all on the area in which L.S.T.424 was wallowing her way forward.

Nerves stretched like piano wire and stomachs churning. The briefing had indicated heavily mined beaches, and it was not considered that the Germans and Italians would yield ground without the utmost resistance having been pushed out of North Africa. It should be noted that although we were not aware of it at the time, the enemy defensive forces on the island at the time of landing numbered 315,000 Italians and 90,000 Germans, some of which were crack units.

Three miles away from the beach we were issued with Thompson sub-machine guns with round pans, and Colt .45 automatics. We were sure, at the time that these had been sent by the FBI who had in turn acquired them from people like Al Capone, Legs Diamond, Dutch

Schultz and Machine Gun Kelly! During night watches on passage, I, like the rest of the party, had learned to strip and re-assemble both guns in complete darkness. We split up into two groups and went over the side onto our respective pontoons, which as I said, had managed to remain secured to the ship against all the odds during the tremendous storms we had sailed through. Approaching the shore at about 10 knots the L.S.T. stopped engines and then went full astern. We slipped the towing lines the instant they slackened. As we shot forward of the ship we could see the other pontoon and heaving lines went both ways. We were lucky first time and the two were pulled together. I went to the forward end of the starboard pontoon with 3 others. Two shore anchors were to be run out at 45 degrees as soon as we beached. One man carries the anchor and the other covers him and makes sure the anchor is secured, and then both hold the beach head thus secured. The same thing of course happens with the other anchor. Meanwhile two kedge anchors had been dropped from the other pontoon as it came in to check it one pontoon length from the shore. The lads still on the causeways warp them into an overlap position and bolt them together. That done, two more guns come to support the beach anchor men. At this point I suddenly realised that no one had as yet taken a shot at us! I had a careful look all round and still no shooting, so L.S.T.424, which had been standing off is signalled that the beach head was secured and unloading can begin.

She immediately moves in, and so does the first STUKA! It screams like a banshee as it builds up speed, and though we 18 year old "veterans" had heard it all before off the coast of North Africa, it was a terrifying sound, and we scrabbled frantically to burrow into the sand. As the noise increased we could not help looking at the sudden death hurtling towards us. The bomb left the plane so close to us that the detonating spike sticking from the nose was clearly visible. The plane skimmed the beach as it clawed desperately for height to climb back to the sky. Luckily for us, he had started his levelling fractionally before the bomb released, and it exploded with a tremendous crash about 40 yards beyond the port anchor. Covered in sand and dust and rubble, with ears and head ringing, it came as something of a surprise to find that neither I nor any other of our party had suffered any injury. By this time, L.S.T.424 was close to the seaward end of the causeway with her bow doors open and the ramp already half lowered. Also at this time the second Stuka came in! Or maybe it was the first one back for a second try. We neither knew nor cared about such academic distinctions. As the diving scream began to wind up, another shape took form behind it my ·first thoughts were, *My God they are queuing up!*

Wrong. It was a Seafire from some ship in that massive convoy, and a sense of relief flooded over me. Wrong again. The Stuka was aiming for us and shooting as he came. The Seafire was aiming for the Stuka and firing eight Brownings simultaneously. Sand was spurting up all around us − holes were appearing noisily in the pontoons, and it sounded like hell let loose. Smoke suddenly appeared from the German plane just as his bomb was released. This time he had been put well off his aim and the bomb exploded 200 yards up the beach. Still no one hurt!

Then the sniping started from the trees 500 yards

inland. A Thompson is fine in a small room for close combat (I've even seen one used to cut down a tree) but it's absolutely useless beyond 30 yards, so it was heads down time again. The two bow Oerlikons from 424 soon quietened the snipers, and the long business of unloading anything that came to our beach began. I realise, at this point, that the way we were organised has not yet been mentioned. It was simply hit the beach and make yourself useful when the initial assault is successful. No provision had been made in this or our other landings for a formal supply system. In short, the little matter of feeding us had never been included in the planning! Certainly we carried 24 hour K-rations initially, but thereon in we had to live off the land or scrounge whatever we could from the army. We never, I must confess, went hungry. There were, I'm sure, many officers messes of all services who wondered why their supplies were always short, but by and large, we always ate (and drank) well. Water that is, because although we 'acquired' plenty of wines and spirits, water was brought in by ship because most supplies had been poisoned by the retreating enemy. Although the Americans had apparently landed on heavily-mined beaches, and the British to our right were also on a mined area, our own beach (Acid North – HOW) turned out to be clean. At least no mines were found that I remember although the first Engineers ashore did sweep it.

On the night of D-Day (10/7/43), Paratroops were flown in and whilst some were dropped in the sea, others dropped in front of our lines and were fired on, unfortunately by our own forces. Another drop caused an incident, of which more shortly.

L.S.T. 424 had gone on its way to Africa for more troops and supplies, so we were now living in Pup Tents in a lemon grove just over the scrub line. Landing went on for five days before easing off. Air attacks were spasmodic, and as the initial frenzied activity slowed to a trickle, we found time to look around and wander further afield. One day, a 4 ring R.N. Captain, in battledress like us of course, asked our C.O. to send out a patrol and requisition a vehicle for him. Even corporals in the Yankee Army had jeeps, so he reckoned he should too. Guess who won the job?!

With three others, I set off, with no clear ideas about how to steal a jeep. All local vehicles had been wrecked and booby-trapped just in case anyone decided to try and mobilise them again. We managed to hitch a lift on a supply truck just ashore and got to Syracuse. I figured there was no way I was about to try and steal a jeep with a lot of trigger happy Americans about. They were great at bragging and shouting, but pathetic when it came to real fighting and holding a beach (this I didn't find out until later, and I would exempt from that statement the U.S. Rangers, who were certainly as good as anything we had). We thought if we stayed away from camp long enough the 'Mad Captain' would have moved on to upset someone else.

Finding a Sicilian barbershop open we had the luxury of a shave and haircut. Not being too sure which side the Sicilians were on, the colt automatics were demonstrably ready. Not needed of course, and we did pay, even if it was only in B.M.A. (British Military Authority) notes. When we came out, we smelled like what in those days was colloquially known as "The clerical assistant to a love-measles specialist" or words to that effect. If your education has not been thorough enough, perhaps, to cover the naval vernacular, the phrase is much more direct – "A pox doctor's clerk!"

It was a long walk back to camp along a dusty rutted road, under a hot July sun, and it was with much relief, that we eventually got a lift on a 10-ton MACK with trailer heading back to the beach supply dumps. I must admit he drove it a damn sight better than I had back in Philippeville!

When we got back to the camp, our C.O. was not in the least surprised to see no jeep, and the "Mad Captain" had sure enough, disappeared. The neat and tidy haircuts, obvious even beneath all the dust, aroused much more interest, and indeed comment. He proceeded, (incidentally, he was known as "Tubby," for obvious reasons) to lecture us on the dangers involved in what we had done. It seemed on the grapevine that two British Soldiers had been found in a flood ditch with their throats cut. They had last been seen heading for a barbershop in Syracuse! It is much more likely that if there was any truth in the story, they had run into a Recce patrol, but such apocryphal stories were common at the time.

During our absence, an Italian machine gun had been found by some of the others, together with plenty of ammunition. Abandoned in a hurry, no doubt, and our lads had lugged it back to camp as a much better defensive proposition than a few Thompsons. They had also found numerous little "butterfly" bombs in the trees and bushes, together with impact bombs (Red Devils I think they were called), placed where they would fall if disturbed and detonate.

Fortunately, they had enough "nouse" to leave them alone, because intriguing as they looked, they would have exploded at the slightest provocation and filled the surrounding air (and people) with all manner of unpleasant things like tacks, nails, ball bearings and broken glass! I suppose we were lucky in that the troops we brought across from Africa had whiled away the evenings regaling us with some of the unfriendly methods the Germans used to discourage people. Particularly nasty little habits like booby-trapping toilets, water pumps, wine bottles, and dead bodies!

We had been on the beach many days now and still nobody hurt! During one night (midnight to 4 a.m.), our middle watch sentries alerted us to aircraft coming in low. Someone had the bright idea that this would be a good time to test the Italian M/C gun. This was duly done as one plane seemed to come in directly towards us. Now these Italian guns fired almost as rapidly as a Spandau, and used a lot of greenish looking tracer in the ammunition mix. In other words they were very easily identifiable as enemy fire by anyone on our side. The planes disappeared northwards, so far as we know, unharmed, but as dawn broke we discovered we were being called upon to surrender!

It was a very British voice, so one of our party, in choice Glaswegian vernacular invited the voice to – er – 'go forth and multiply' as it were! After a nonplussed silence, in which all Thompsons were carefully released from safe, a cautious head was raised, and the polite enquiry, "Who the hell are you?" was made. When many British voices answered in a collection of crude but definitive adjectives, more heads rose all round us, each supported by a body bristling with assorted instruments of mayhem.

It appeared that (again unknown to us – one rarely, if ever, knew what was happening outside of immediate rifle range) the Germans had moved north and were making a heavy and determined stand at Catania. Airborne troops had been flown in during the night to reinforce our spearhead to break them. One highly irritated pilot had reported being fired on by Italian partisans whilst flying low over country he had been assured was cleared of all enemy!

Our attackers had been dispatched to mop up the "guerrilla outpost!" They were actually Black Watch, although they were not themselves Scots, and after much muttering about 'bloody matelots playing at soldiers' the sergeant in charge took his force and disappeared north at a fast rate of knots. Not, I'm afraid, before he had 'neutralised' our Italian M/C gun with a couple of grenades: "To avoid," he said, "any further misunderstandings." After that, we just sunbathed and wandered around the olive groves, or picked walnuts and lemons.

We were on the beach, as near as I can remember, for about 10 days, and then L.S.T. 424 came back and we tied our causeways alongside, picked up our monkeys and parrots, and fell in three deep facing the boat. Metaphorically, that is, since the role we were filling demanded implicit discipline in operational situations but tended to undermine the bullshit parade ground sort. Incidentally, I was uprated from Ordinary Seaman to Seaman on 15th July 1943. This is equivalent to A.B. in General Service, and was actually pretty good going, because I had only been in the 'Andrew' for six months, and in peacetime it took between 12 months and 2 years. Despite our Commando status, we were still R.N.P.S. (Royal Navy Patrol Service) and, I might add, proud of it. Most of our R.N.P.S. ships were built of wood. Particularly if they were new and function built, to be able to sweep for magnetic as well as all the other types of mine. When General Service types were met we seldom failed to remind them that, as in Nelson's time, it was always a question, Wooden ships – Ironmen, or in General Service, Iron ships – Wooden men! It never went down very well with them for some reason, but by and large honours were even and the bruises soon faded.

For the next few weeks we sculled around the Mediterranean, mainly along the North African coast. We were working up our landing techniques, learning something about explosives, and sailing in and out of all sorts of bays along the coast. At some time or other (not necessarily during these few weeks), we must have called in on almost every coastal hamlet east of Algiers through to Tripoli. Our shallow draft meant we could go into many places that had never seen anything larger than a small fishing boat. Bougie (now Bougea) I have already mentioned, some others I recall are Sousse, Sfax, Bone, Philippeville and Bizerta. There were of course, others whose names escape me, and some whose names I never knew. Tiny groups of broken down clay buildings with corrugated roofs and lean-to shelters for the stragglylooking sheep or goats. The half-naked children knew how to call "Baksheesh Jonnie Baksheesh!" There were skinny dogs with ribs sticking out of almost hairless bodies, and idle Arabs lolling about in dirty Djellabas, while the women cooked and fetched water from ancient-looking wells, probably bored by the Romans. The wells that is! The men were rarely seen to move but anything left unattended seemed to vanish as if by magic. Frequently it was offered for sale, even to its original owner if he still happened to be around – one of the reasons for the stories around, about the British ill-treating the local inhabitants!

We lost spanners, sylvesters, nuts, bolts, welding tackle, and personal possessions without ever seeing them go. In consequence we were not too disturbed by conscience when we bartered tins of tea for fresh eggs. The top layer of tea was OK, but below the first inch, it had all been retrieved from the tea kettles after we had brewed up.

We were offered on one occasion a large box containing nuts, bolts (by some coincidence exactly the size used on our causeway), two sylvesters, one four foot spanner, and a selection of battledress blouses without any identifying badges of course. We bartered for them with blankets (with which we were all issued – it gets very cold at nights in those parts), all clearly marked R.N. 200yds down the road the perimeter patrol stopped the Arabs and confiscated the blankets they had obviously stolen since they were marked R.N.! The Arabs were last seen heading for the desert faster than I'd ever seen them move, having been warned they would be shot on sight if seen again. Quite an empty threat as we could not tell one from the other anyway. The blankets were then returned to their owners.

Towards the end of August the continual training eased off. I was given the chance, whilst we were at sea, of acting as quartermaster's mate. In practice this meant, apart from being general dogsbody, messenger and runabout, I actually got to take a spell on the wheel. This was great, and I really enjoyed it until the Skipper, whose name I never did know, called down the voice pipe, "I would prefer you not to go back to dot the i's helmsman, and that thing floating in the binnacle is called a compass. Moreover, if you look at it occasionally you will find that the course I asked you to steer is definitely there somewhere!" This because I was half a degree off course! He was nevertheless a good Skipper.

My normal battle station was on the starboard Oerlikon in the bows, and we had some very pleasant practices shooting at loose mines and occasionally sharks (hammerheads) or seagulls. The mines I could hit, the others were much more difficult. I certainly never hit one and I cannot recall anyone else doing so either.

More pleasant memories return of the L.S.T. heaving to in the middle of the Mediterranean and hands piped to bathe. Action stations was always piped on these occasions because although the draught was too shallow for submarines to torpedo us (or so we thought), they could surface and engage us in gun actions, and their deck guns invariably out-ranged our twelve pounder on the stern. Nor did we wish to be caught unawares by aircraft. In addition, the hammerhead sharks were reputed not to attack humans unless trapped in harbours or shallow waters, but our Skipper was not at all sure if the sharks were aware of this reputation. We therefore had a shark watch covering the swimmers. This consisted of two rifles and two Thompson sub-machine guns. The rifles were fine but God help us if ever the Thompsons were called upon to fire.

As it turned out, the only time they did we were all back inboard. The procedure was to open the bow doors and lower the ramp to sea level. This way, we had no need of Jacob's ladder or scrambling nets to get back aboard. After swimming had gone on for a while, "Sharks!" was called. Everyone made hell-for-leather for the ramp. I have never been either a good swimmer or a fast one, but I was not the last to the ramp! On the alarm being raised, the Skipper had walked to the bows and relieved the Starboard Tommy gunner of his weapon. "No one fires until I give the word," he said. The shark was certainly there, more, I suspect, in a spirit of curiosity than with any carnivorous intent.

However, once the Skipper spotted it he blazed away with the Thompson at a range of at least 100 yards, which meant there was no way he could reach it. The splashes, fifty yards short, had started well to the left of the shark and sprayed leftwards away from it, and were in grave danger of cutting the jackstay down!

Everyone else around had immediately hit the deck. Very wise too. When the pan was empty, the Skipper returned the gun to its original guardian (by this time rising to his feet) and suggested anyone else of the watch who cared to might also have a go. The whole watch immediately opened fire, but the shark apparently bored with the whole proceedings swam immediately away unharmed.

During this period of sculling around up and down the North African coastline, we had several practice night runs on which we, "Party Cable," were dropped in rubber assault boats a couple of miles offshore. We were to land

47

on beaches (previously closely studied on the charts), split into three groups, and reconnoitre a quarter of a mile inland. Having done this, return to the water-line, open up to a mile apart, and show red and green lights at the extremities and a white one in the centre. These trips were always made with full combat equipment, including the usual Thompsons and Colts together with hand grenades and explosives. Knives, compass in buttons, saw blades in lanyards, and screw on boot heels which usually carried a second compass, and a 'don't talk' pill, sometimes called 'L' pills,[5] presumably because they would be the last one you would ever take. They were white and square so as not to be confused with anything else and were, I believe, pure cyanide. I later learned that the SOE and OSS people had 'Q' pills, which were actually little glass phials of a milky white liquid, again cyanide.

The lanyard was the only part of naval uniform worn, and it was beneath the battledress blouse, its purpose was for cutting through steel wire or garrotting as required. It did not take long for the purpose of this training to be recognised, because although we were young and naive, we were not entirely muscle-bound between the ears. Thinking about the 'L' pills I'm not so sure about this! It didn't strike me, or I think any of the others, until a long time after these events that something didn't add up. We were beach assault groups who could be used for any job, either in, from or behind the lines, but what did we know that could possibly warrant an 'L' pill? I've never heard of the regular commando units carrying them. The conclusion I eventually came to was that someone at some

---

[5] 'L also = LETHAL

time had perhaps intended us being dropped on a wrong beach at a wrong time to persuade the Germans into pulling troops away from the right ones. Taking them on training jaunts was to get us used to the idea that they were standard kit.

I never did know what the truth of it was (I was not aware at that time that Hitler had said earlier in the war that any Commando prisoners taken were to be killed). We were being trained to hit the enemy beaches before the main invasion forces, and ensure they came in at the right place! Charming! Oh well, if you can't take a joke you shouldn't have joined.

The idea of carrying out this sort of operation was reinforced by having our own Army units patrolling our practice beaches without telling them we were coming! We learned to be very, very quiet in our work! Actually, I believe it worked in our favour and none of our people were hurt. This was because we realised the obvious, silence was probably the only thing that would keep us alive when we did it for real. The Army patrols were well informed on the course of the war, and had no reason to suppose that the enemy would attempt to come back to Africa, at least while they had their hands full in Italy. Consequently they were always relatively noisy, grumbling about useless night patrols on deserted beaches miles from any possible target. We were thus always able to locate their passing, and wait until our signals would be made. Leading Seaman Whitmore pointed out to us that we could not expect the Germans to be so accommodating.

Shortly after this I was summoned late one evening and informed I was required by the Admiral's staff, at that time in Sousse. The reason given was that an air raid had killed and injured some of the writers and some devious character had seen on my record that I had studied shorthand and typing whilst with the Police.

On arrival at Sousse, the first thing I had to do was sign the Official Secrets Act document. It was late and they found me a corner to sleep in. My typing was of the slow, two fingered variety and my shorthand was frequently not understood. By me as well as others! I need not have worried! In the morning, a Sub Lt. R.N. (dressed in khaki battledress of course) rousted me out and on the way to the mess hall (we all ate together) told me he was one short for his 'holiday cruise' and asking around had heard of our little jolly in Sicily. A word or two in the right ears and the order had been given – 'Send me one with enough nouse for a swift in/out job!' Now we know where the short straw was! Someone once said, "Energy and confidence are the currency of youth." If that's true, it seems someone was after my cash!

After breakfast, we were ferried out to a submarine in the bay. No sooner aboard than we slipped out of the bay and dived. It was no consolation that no one had ever said that we had to like it! This, we thought, looked more of a serious exercise or perhaps?? The narrow walkways festooned with dozens of pipes against which we were frequently jammed as the crew answered the alarm klaxon, the air smelling of diesel, cabbage and unwashed bodies, and the knowledge that there was only one way out, did nothing for my claustrophobia. We sailed for five days never knowing where we were until we were finally told that a standby patrol was needed for a beach on the Italian mainland. Did this mean that the next, much talked of landings were on?

We were then briefed that we should know what was required of us and nothing more. The less we knew, the less we could ....er...yield to the persuasive, if barbaric methods the Germans were then using. The boat lay on the bottom all of the sixth day. It surfaced at night and we waited with blacked faces, churning guts, and nerves stretched like bow strings. I can only speak for myself when I say that at these times the waiting was agonising, and knowing there were no longer any choices for me, I would sooner get on with it. I've always had my fair share of imagination, and the tension built up in the waiting period was not only the fear of being killed or injured (and that was certainly there), but also the fear of discovering that one couldn't do it, of letting the others down, in short, of being a coward. I discovered quite early that all the brave and courageous men I met (and in that kind of business you met quite a few) were not ashamed to admit being afraid before they went in on these and similar occasions. I also discovered a little later that being aware of this and, to some extent comforted, that I was not alone in my fears, it didn't help one iota the next time I had to do it, or the next! But I digress. Waiting below the forward loading hatch, already opened, I tried to look as controlled and prepared as the others looked. After half an hour of checking and rechecking all working mechanisms and equipment, the hatch suddenly clanged shut from above and we were dived and moving in minutes. We were stood down and told we were not required this time but no reason was given, and I never knew where we had almost gone ashore.

Submarines are not equipped with many toilets and, because of the peculiarities of flushing them (to do with equalising pressures without and within, this I think also applies to the reason for needing them, although there was certainly a metal one in there somewhere – very messy if you get it wrong), the sudden demand created quite a queue.

We were disembarked from the submarine (and I felt a relief which had nothing to do with the operation we had been planned for – I was in the open again) and re-united with L.S.T. 424. I need hardly add that I was treated like a hero, extra tots and 'sippers' all round, and the crew simply would not believe I had done nothing. They were convinced I had been sworn to secrecy and many ploys were tried to find out what the operation had been. Eventually the number of different 'accounts' they had 'ferreted' out almost convinced them I was telling the truth. But never completely!

We sailed for Bizerte and once more began loading troops and vehicles. Not tanks. Once again, the destination was a closely guarded secret until we were well out to sea and on the way. It appears it hadn't been kept so well from the Germans as we were to discover! The cruise was relatively uneventful and, as on the last operation, Party Cable was excused all sea-going duties. This, and the free cigarettes we were issued filled us once more with the same apprehension, fears, nerves – call it what you will – as we had experienced at Sicily. This time though, we had one landing on enemy beaches under our belts, and were not the same green boys who had thought wars to be some sort of glamorous game. Relatively

52

painless as our first landing had been, we had seen that this business (it was never a game) was deadly serious and played for keeps.

1943 Lovat

I have to assume this happened sometime in late 1943.

One day, I was ironing my white shirts ready for getting out of khaki and back into naval rig. (I thought at that time. As it turned out this did not happen for a long time.)

A corporal of Commando's came in and said, "Oooh you'll make someone a nice wife!" I suppose I must have been intolerant that particular morning since I assumed he was saying that ironing was a woman's job.

All I said was: "Watch your lips corporal, they are flapping and I might have to secure them!" Needless to say, he put me on a charge. The Lieutenant, whose name I don't remember, said, "What exactly did you say?" So I told him and he put me on a charge as well! That meant, in our camp, going in front of Lord Lovat. When that occasion arrived (he wasn't always in camp), he asked what the charge was and was told it was insolent and threatening behaviour. (I should point out that reflection suggested I would not have made much of a dent in a guy whose training in the arts of close combat was much more comprehensive than mine.) When his Lordship had heard the detail, he said, "For God's sake, Lieutenant, what the hell do you think we've been training them to be?"

"Case dismissed," he said, "and Lieutenant, I suggest you look around for a situation more suited to your temperament!" Unusual, to say the least, for a Senior Officer to make any sort of derogatory remark to one of his officers in front of a lower rank but he followed it up with: "And you, boy, control your temper or you'll certainly find the sort of trouble you won't be able to handle!"

I have no idea what happened but I never saw the guy again and the unfortunate corporal was killed on our next raid. I don't think he really meant to imply that I was effeminate but, to my shame, I admit I had bad days too.

Not only that, I'm not even sure it was Lord Lovat I saw. He looked nothing like his later television appearances. Whoever it was he certainly had a lot of clout where it mattered. This must have occurred sometime after the Bone submarine incident I suppose but too much time has passed since those days and I simply can't remember! The events yes, but where it fits in time has gone.

Before we were told where we were going to land for our second time, we began to get curious about what sort of odds we could expect on surviving a second beach assault.

I have since discovered that the odds we could expect on surviving one assault were in the order of 2 to 1 against, surviving two assaults 10 to 1, and surviving three 25 to 1. It was all hypothetical, since it depended on how well the beach was defended and how long they had known we were coming. Even if the secret had been kept successfully as to where the exact location would be, all practical beach landing possibilities were heavily mined, covered with pill boxes and machine gun posts to give cross-fire, closely guarded and linked by field telephone to inland airfields. Under water obstructions were placed and mined, and knowing all these things we rated our own chances at much less than 50/50. I imagine looking back, that the only way we lived with that at the time was not through any stupid bravado, but simply that each and every man convinced himself that he would be amongst the few who did survive. It's never you but the bloke next to you who gets it when the imagination takes you up the beach hours before zero hour.

Guns stripped and cleaned (again) and reassembled, letters to be written (though many believed if they didn't write farewell letters they would be OK), I had no particular beliefs one way or the other as far as superstition was concerned. I had written one farewell letter before the first landing in Sicily, and only finally destroyed it when a troopship dropped me in Greenock alongside a railway coal wagon marked MALTBY.

We were still conjecturing on whether we would be going in as beach markers this time but no clues were forthcoming. We had all the necessary gear, and it would have been simple to transfer us to something fast enough to arrive before the Convoy. Again, with hindsight I am eternally grateful that they didn't. Nothing happened until the Tannoy opened up with – "Do you hear there, do you hear there. This is the Captain speaking. I can now tell you that we shall, in the early hours of the morning, be landing you on the beaches near a town called SALERNO." Codenamed 'Avalanche' the Salerno landings were described by Churchill as 'the most daring we have yet launched.' "Report to your own C.O.'s for briefing, and

God go with you. That is all, except their Lordships have instructed me to 'splice the mainbrace' – this includes all ranks and U.A.'s[6] and of course our Army friends."

Amazing when you think about it that we were old enough at 18 to land on enemy beaches and perhaps get quite messily killed, but their Lordships in their wisdom considered that allowing us a rum ration was putting our immortal souls in unacceptable danger! Except in special circumstances of course! One was not normally entitled to a rum issue each day until the age of 21.

It was very obvious as we neared the coastline in the early hours of the morning that this was a totally different kettle of fish to Sicily. Shore batteries had engaged our rocket firing LCT's as they moved in to lay a beach blaster down. Each LCT fired a pattern of rockets (HE heads with a 29lb charge and 7lb bursters), which were pre-set to cover 750yds of beach to a strip 160yds deep, supposed to clear mines and people off enough of the beach so we could get a fingernail grip on it. They were fired in 24 salvos of 6 by electrical triggers, and looked extremely impressive from our end. Didn't fancy seeing them from the other end! Cruisers and Destroyers laid down a barrage further inland, and laid smoke inshore. We were not riding the pontoons in on this trip although they had come with us and were to be used later. L.S.T. 424 dropped her kedge anchor and drove through the smoke, bow doors open and ramp half down. She hit with a shuddering jolt and the ramp dropped and I was running up Salerno Beach on 10th September 1943. There was smoke and noise everywhere; shells bursting both in the

---

[6]Underage for rum issue.

air and on the beach. M/C Guns were kicking sand up all around us and there was the angry whine of ricochets. My feet suddenly went from under me as I stumbled over an obstruction and hit the beach with a thud that knocked the wind out of me and it sounded like a swarm of angry hornets swept over my head. I never knew his name, but he had been wearing a green beret and the previous sweep of that M/C gun had stitched a deadly line across his chest. He had saved my life by being where he was as the gun swept back on its reverse traverse. Nausea held me pressed to the ground while my breathing steadied. It was in fact, one of those moments when nothing in one's body could be trusted to work without intense personal supervision, but I knew I must make my 200yds and I crawled on until I reached the scrub dunes. Something moved ahead and I fired, somewhat wildly at it. It was reassuring to hear firing from right and left as well, and then two grenades exploded in sharp succession and the M/C gun fell silent.

We had landed with a reception committee of dug-in 88mm self-propelled guns backed up by tanks. To our left the US Rangers were engaged in heavy fighting as their rockets had been fired on the wrong beach so the enemy had not been softened-up for them.

We were regrouped and Tubby led us half a mile inland. We were then ordered back to the beach to secure the causeway because air attacks and shelling were taking too much toll of ships on the beach, and it was considered that swift one-at-a-time runs to the causeway would be easier to defend. I was not so sure myself! Whilst we had cruisers lying off and taking on tanks when they could be spotted, we had no forward observers to direct the fire in a decisive way. By nightfall no ships were coming in, but plenty of shells were, and we crouched in our shallow foxholes to avoid the shrapnel. I suppose we must have dozed intermittently even in that din, because suddenly it was dawn again. K-rations and water had been left by 424 for us when we secured the pontoons, and we snatched a furtive breakfast.

As the first ship approached, the firing and the din suddenly increased behind us (inland). We were immediately regrouped and set off back inland. Coming up with the Army lads about three quarters of a mile in, we found the Germans were making a very heavy counterattack. We used everything we had and fell back to where ammunition was waiting. Then we did it again, and this time we could hear the surf behind us between the bangs. The 'express trains' started coming over above us from the cruisers, and only that bombardment saved the beach. When the beachhead had been pushed to half mile again, we returned once again to landing duties. This to-ing and fro-ing went on for seven days and nights, and on one occasion we got a lift on a D.U.K.W with supplies to the front, which was, we were told, about a mile away. Rounding a dune we came face to face with a Tiger tank, who fortunately, was as surprised as us and rather slower off the mark. It seemed the line was not a mile away! For reasons best known to himself he didn't follow us, although we spread out and dug in knowing we couldn't outrun him. Round about D+9, the Germans withdrew but only in front of the beachhead, but prior to that the Yanks to our right had pulled off the beach one night and left us exposed on the flank. There must have been some radio communication somewhere because the Rangers slipped through us from the other side and plugged the hole.

It was round about this time when the Germans first made a concentrated use of radio-controlled bombs. This resulted in the Battleship Warspite and the Cruiser Uganda being put out of action, as well as the American's Philadelphia and Savannah. The bombers came over very high, well out of range of any of our guns, and in the clear Mediterranean air simply steered their bombs to the targets, much like today's model planes. They were quite callous about the targets, and we watched the Hospital ship (St. David, I believe) attacked and destroyed only a mile off shore. She was painted brilliant white with massive red crosses on her sides and deck, and could not possibly have been mistaken for anything but what she was. Records will show that no prisoners were taken for the next few days!

Our next orders lifted us off the beach to an American tug who fed us in true American style, better than we had eaten for a long time. When we discovered what was required of us, we wondered if it was a case of the condemned man eating a hearty breakfast. It appeared that no American could be sent overseas to what was described as a 'theatre of war' unless he was not less than twenty-one years. They were astounded that eighteen year olds were doing commando operations. You will recall that I mentioned the enemy had fallen back from the beachhead. No-one, it seemed, knew whether he was still holding the town of Salerno, and the High Command decided we should find out. The purpose was to install our pontoons alongside the damaged jetties to facilitate faster movement of supplies to our hard pressed troops.

The tug slipped in through the protective sea wall and

dropped us on the inner wall across the harbour front, about 2am, and then slipped out again. Tubby held us until dawn, explaining that if the Germans were still there, they had all the advantages, and our little twenty strong strike force was a reconnaissance, not a suicide squad. We manned our rubber boats as the light increased, and began to paddle as quietly as possible across the harbour. The first shells fell in the town before us, and we thought our supporting destroyers were softening things up for us. Then the shells began to come towards us, and we did a rapid change of direction back to the sea wall as we recognised that the Germans were in the hills just above the town, and seeing us quite clearly, were ranging in on us. We scrambled in an undignified manner over the top of the sea wall to the seaward side and were very grateful it was so thick. By midday the destroyers had finally caught on to what was happening and put a fierce barrage on the hills. Everything quietened down after an hour or so, and Tubby sent Blackie and five of us to check the town and the jetties, in the belief that there was not likely to be any more resistance.

We had to make our way the long way round, along the sea wall since the rubber boats had gone almost as soon as we were scrambling to safety that morning. We were not left in doubt for long: mortar shells began dropping at the town end of the wall and creeping out towards us. We dropped back from cover to cover as well as we could, one can't fight mortars with a 'Tommy Gun'. After some time, we eventually regained our original position facing out to sea. Efforts were made to signal to the ships offshore but no answers were seen. It looked as if we were trapped on the mole, and though it seemed

61

unlikely the Germans would try to take us, it seemed equally unlikely we could get into the town to have a go at them. The afternoon dragged on with salvos from the German 88's forcing our heads down every time we tried to move, followed by salvos from the sea as our ships tried to silence the 88's. No chance really since they were mobile.

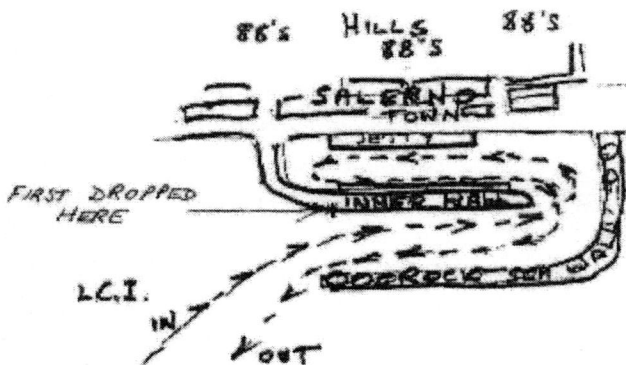

As dusk fell an L.C. I. made a gallant run in to take us off. (It was not until afterwards we learned the L.C.I. had been detached from duty because she only had one engine working. Repairs to the other were suspended by her skipper when he was informed that he was the only thing small enough and near enough to get us out.) She had to run through the entrance walls parallel to the town, then back on the inner side, turn and pause close to the wall to lift us off. Shells were falling all around her as we leapt for the scrambling nets as she brushed the wall past us. Then we were on and she opened up to make the same perilous run out again. It seemed miraculous that none of those shells actually hit her, but they were very, very close.

We were taken back and dropped at our beach base, and similarly the idea of using the pontoons in the harbour was also dropped. Until the hills commanding the harbour were taken, it was not a viable plan, and when they were it would be too late to give any advantage. We remained on the beach for a few more days, and it was obvious that the previous fortnight had taken its toll. Mugs tended to rattle against teeth, and tea was spilled from shaking hands. We had always worked well as a group but now tempers were short and flared for no apparent reason. It seemed 'Party Cable', had some damaged links and was no longer an effective operational unit.

A destroyer, of whose name I have no recollection, lifted us from the beach, and we were ferried to Malta. Put ashore there, we were billeted in Verdala barracks, which in peace time had been a prison. Apart from the usual 'steal' from Dante – "Abandon hope all ye who enter here" – which decorated the entrance archway, I found the most magnificent carving around one of the stone columns. It consisted of a winding road climbing the column and at each full wind a different house or dwelling in minute detail. The bottom one was a simple cottage (Mediterranean style of course), and each one was a little more ornate. The top one was a beautiful Palace with columns, courtyards and waterfalls in bas-relief. The name of the long-term prisoner, whose days, weeks, and years it had occupied, I was unable to discover.

A doctor examined everyone in the party and decided a spell in a "Rest Camp" would perhaps get us back in shape again. It seemed powers that be had not finished with us yet! Whilst I remember, Tubby had decided before the last operation that we ought to carry emergency medical equipment, and someone should be responsible for not only making sure it didn't get lost or find its way to the black market, but also for using it should the need arise. Logical and not unreasonable under the circumstances. What I felt was out of order was that I should get elected! I never did care much for the sight of blood. Particularly mine!

However, that's how it turned out, and I had been lugging a back pack stuffed with wound dressings, scalpels, forceps, splints, sulphanilamide's and Morphine Ampoules and syringes ever since. Apart from issuing mepacrine every day and dressing a few cuts and grazes I never had needed to use it. I'm sure, for their sakes that was a good thing! ('Party Cable' that is.)

We must have been in Malta for two or three weeks because I recollect odd things like staying overnight in a 'hotel' in "The Gut." Playing 'housey housey'[7] in the Governor General's Palace. ("Tiger" Gort held the office at that time, I believe.) I never won, but those that did had a full Naval Shore Patrol escort since the prize money was more than a year's earnings for a seaman at that time. One other thing sticks in my mind from that visit to Malta, and that was drinking in a bar down "The Gut" which was run by two 'queers'. They dressed in women's clothing and looked, I must admit, better than some, in fact most, of the women who were 'plying for hire' in the same area. Why I remember that particular occasion is that a party of matelots who had drunk, not wisely but too well, on the

---

[7] Now known as Bingo

64

rot-gut being sold as whisky made some derogatory remarks about these two 'pseudo ladies'. The remarks were not only impolite, they were crude and provocative. The 'ladies' invited the matelots to leave as they would get no more to drink there. The response to 'go forth and multiply' as it were, led to one of the most efficient and clinical evictions I have ever seen. The two 'ladies' took on ten matelots and in less than five minutes had laid out six and ejected four to the roadway with hardly a false eyelash out of place. I was very pleased to be an observer rather than a participant, and my calls of 'Bravo' earned me a free drink on the house. A valuable lesson had been learned. My upbringing had been, I thought, a natural and normal one, but I had not realised how sheltered it had been from the realities of life. Those two characters had taught me sharply and succinctly, that people may assume a mantle they preferred to the one they were born with, but that did not for one moment negate the physical attributes that their original state had endowed them with, or indeed, the will to protect their chosen life.

Back to Verdala, and the following morning (I think) we were embarked on a L.S.T., which I believe was 414 but I can't be sure. It was only when we left Malta and ran into engine trouble that I realised we were not the only cripples heading for Tripoli and maintenance. Being reduced to one engine and not, therefore, able to keep pace with the already slow convoy, we were taken in tow by a destroyer.

This was enough excitement for the day so I turned in. After all, we were 'Rest Camp' candidates, and not expected at that stage to take any active part in whatever bit of war was going on in our theatre.

Dragged, unmercifully, from my bunk, and from a deep and dreamless sleep, I struggled to understand the shouted information being directed to me. "Wake up you stupid bastard (a term of affection), we've been torpedoed." The word 'torpedoed' triggered some instinctive and primeval reaction in my battered brain, and I shot out of my bunk, along the bunk space, and out to the upper deck like a bat out of hell. It was only when I had been there for long enough to see that we were still floating, albeit with a list, and that our towing destroyer was not only not towing, but not in sight, that I realised I had nothing on my feet.

It was a long, long time since I had undressed to go to bed, but one thing that did come off was footwear. I know sailors are supposed to sing sea shanties whilst swabbing the decks with bare feet, but not on steel decks! The torpedo had hit on the waterline and almost dead centre. It had gone clean through the heads, and exploded in the tank space. Most of the blast had gone upwards and ripped a massive, jagged hole in the top deck. The deck lurched under my stockinged feet, and the starboard rail was now very close to the water, a voice from the stern shouted "Abandon ship!" (I learned later that the order to abandon ship had not been given by the C.O.), and then much shouting occurred which I couldn't decipher. It looked easy to step off the starboard side into the water, but when I looked across the deck it was looming over me as though it was about to roll over and reminded me all too clearly of the Polish-manned L.S.T. turning turtle, so I thought the port side would be better. Scrambling up that sloping deck was not easy, and when I reached the port rail I hung on and took a look down. It looked a long way to the water, and all the welds stuck up where the plates were joined. I thought if I go down there I shall have a ripped bum as the least of my problems, and had the immediate, fleeting thought as to whether the hammerhead sharks would make the distinction that this was human blood and they weren't supposed to find out if the source of it was threatening them, so I then decided that the bow was the best place to be and set off accordingly. As I reached the bow, the thought occurred to me that I had been messing about for some considerable time and the ship hadn't sunk yet! I had seen and heard many people going into the water, and the Carley floats had been launched. A lot of shouting was still going on and the people seemed to be close to the ship, both in the water and on the floats. A lad from near Halifax was with me at the bow (a later flash of memory recalls his name as Gerry Marshall, but I couldn't be sure). Another name comes to mind for his mate Derek Sandown. We had decided to stay put until something else happened which would indicate it would be healthier to move. Suddenly the single good engine started up and the ship shuddered and began to surge in a wide circle. Screams came from the water as the screw pulled in anything or anybody near enough. Tubby appeared and we were 'volunteered' to go below and stop the engine. Each watertight door was closed behind us, and as I dogged them secure I could feel the sense of claustrophobia strengthening. There was only one thing for it and that was to get to the engine room fast, stop the engine, and get back up top even faster. I was convincing myself, remembering again the Polish ship on the way to Sicily that we should have rolled over long before that but somehow I managed to keep going.

At the engine room we were met by a leading stoker, singing for all he was worth, and with a bottle of rum in one hand. Tubby's order, after one look, was brief – "Take him out." (I should point out that we were well aware that Tubby had not meant a terminal 'taking out', which of course we had been trained to do.) That was not an invitation to go walking, and we dropped him to the deck as Tubby slammed the clutch out and stopped the generator. I wished he had left it running because it knocked out the lights and left only pale blue emergency lighting. We got out as fast as we could, and the smell of fresh air, even tainted with fire, explosive and oil, was like the most beautiful scent I've ever smelled. We dragged the unfortunate Stoker through the last hatchway and dogged it shut. Leaving him where he lay, we went forward to the bow again and someone stuck a cigarette in my mouth. By now our towing destroyer had finished its sweep and finding nothing to attack had returned to attempt to tow us once more, whilst two Corvettes were picking up survivors. This of course, was some two hours after we were hit. The ship had settled lower in the water but the bulkheads were holding. We secured the tow quite easily since it was a placid sea, had it not been casualties would have been much higher than they were. The only one of the "Party Cable" to be lost was 'Blackie'. The leading seaman's mess was on the port side, opposite to where I had been, and some weird effect of the blast had ripped across his bunk and killed him instantly, without leaving any sign of injury. It was a bitter blow to us and it seemed unjust somehow, that he should have survived the landings we'd made (and done his damnedest to make sure we survived them as well), only to be killed as a passenger en route to a rest-camp. I have since learned that the man lost was not 'Blackie', who was later awarded a DSM, but a leading seaman named Casper from one of the other Party Cable groups. Many others were lost too, and tragically, some of them due to a mistaken sense of duty by one man starting the engine again.

The rest of the journey was uneventful until we reached Tripoli.

The destroyer slipped the tow as we approached the beach to the left of the harbour. That was when the surviving bulkheads in the tank space finally gave way, and she settled sedately on the bottom with just the superstructure showing. What few of us had remained on board were lifted off and taken to the rest-camp. This refers only to the Party Cable members, and not the passage crew or other passengers. It was a long low building standing in its own grounds by the sea, to the west of the harbour. I've no idea what it had been, but it was fitted out like a luxurious hotel, or perhaps more correctly, sanatorium. At that time, I only recall five of Party Cable being there, and none of us had any idea of whether the rest had survived the torpedo, or been rescued from the water.

We were utterly exhausted both mentally and physically, and although they tried to feed us, coffee was all we could manage before the sight of individual beds with spotless sheets and pillow cases dragged us away from everything. What they put in the coffee I don't know, but it was three days later when I woke to find a drip in my arm. The others were in the same situation, and seeing I was awake if not fully aware, an orderly came over and told me that the drip was intravenous feeding. He took it out and brought me another coffee, this time without the 'mickey'. The cup still rattled against my teeth and I needed both hands to control it, but that gradually disappeared under the care and attention we received. Whilst I was under the original sedation, which I understand was standard procedure for what they called 'battle fatigued' troops (shell-shocked in the previous War) the rest of our party had been brought in. Casper had been buried in a military cemetery, and we were sad not to have carried him ourselves.

We spent nearly three weeks at that rest-camp, doing only what we wished to do, with no restrictions apart from hospital ones relating to bed times etc. The long silvery sanded beach was where most of the day was spent, and the surf there had a very strong undertow, this I found out the hard way! I thought one could dive straight through the big rollers and come out in the calm behind them. The diving bit was fine, but then I felt the roller push me down with tremendous force to the sand below, which I formed with my head. The next thing I knew was someone slapping my face. The undertow had bounced me on my head, knocked me out, and rolled me up the beach where fortunately I was seen before it dragged me back again.

Another 'Mickey Finn' and two more days in bed. Still, at least the nervous twitch had gone, and my hands were back under my control again. Eventually that life of luxury ended and we were called back to the war again.

Another L.S.T. whose number I can't recall, and a lot more runs ferrying troops from Africa and Italy. We, 'Party Cable', had acquired all sorts of souvenirs on these trips. Mostly from Yanks who had bought them from

Arabs when they had first arrived in North Africa fresh from the States. (Everything we had acquired the hard way had been lost when we were torpedoed.)

The Yanks played a lot of poker and many were flat broke and would swap pistols, Nazi knives and helmets for cigarettes. I was not a smoker when I joined the Navy, but I certainly was at this stage. However, the issue of cigarettes we had received at that time were something called 'Victory V's'. Now, although I have never knowingly smoked camel dung, I was assured by my L.R.D.G. and Popski's[8] friends that the similarity was too close for coincidence. Suffice to say that, even under the stresses of our everyday existence, most of us had forsworn the noxious weed. At least until we could get something smokable. (L.R.D.G. = Long Range Desert Group. Popski = leader of desert force operating behind enemy lines, which I believe included in its ranks some of the original S.B.S. and S.A.S. personnel.)

The reason for the little comment on smoking is simply that having cigarettes I didn't want enabled me to do a little bartering, which led to one more of my 'near misses'. My acquisition was a small and neat .22 Beretta pistol. This I exchanged with an officer's steward (Ken Turner – who came from near Sevenoaks, if I remember rightly) for cigarettes from the Wardroom – players, of course. The problem was that when I gave Ken the gun, he raised it, said, "Is it loaded?", and pressed the trigger.

---

[8] I am almost certain that Popski's main bases were in Egypt, but I never went there and I'm equally certain that we met those boys in Phillipeville or Bone. This would be early 1943 and certainly before Sicily.

It was! I got a blinding flash and a blast thump on the face and fell to the deck. The bullet had lodged in the insulation of the pipes in the cold room where our transaction was taking place.

When my sight came back, I could see Ken's white face, in shock as he thought he'd killed me. For an instant, I had thought that too! Feeling a bit peeved, I doubled the price which he was happy to pay.

Later, we laughed over the incident with a bottle of wine (also from the Wardroom), although neither of us had thought it funny at the time.

On one of these ferrying trips, we were required to take troops and supplies to Taranto. I have mentioned how slow the L.S.T.'s were before, and for this reason we had to Heave-to outside the harbour to allow the fast mine-laying Cruiser Welshman to go through first. I have no idea what sort of mine she hit, but her bows were opened up and she just ploughed straight down to the bottom of the harbour. Many lives were lost, but I learned that she was salvaged sometime later and used again, although taking no further part in the war.

It was now late in the year of 1943, which had been a somewhat eventful one both in terms of history and my own personal experiences. Christmas morning was spent on watch steaming towards Tripoli, where I got the opportunity to have a record played on the radio at home. I forget the details, but it was something like Forces Favourites, and it was played on Sunday mornings. No one at home knew where I was or what I was doing because we were not allowed to say, and all mail was censored to make sure we didn't. I figured my Mum was smart enough to work it out for herself if I chose the right music. Knowing we had secured a foothold in Southern Italy, everyone was talking about a big Spring offensive through the soft underbelly of Europe in the newspapers that filtered through to us, I chose Sinding's 'Rustle of Spring'. As luck would have it, it was played shortly after our next beachhead landing (not strictly true in my case since we went into harbour this time, me in particular as you will see) and although they mentioned the name of the requester, they simply said *with the Navy overseas*. Mother told me afterwards she knew immediately where I was because, she said, of my perverse sense of humour!

We didn't move from Tripoli until a couple of weeks into the New Year 1944. Up the coast to the west again, and another load of troops and trucks. We didn't need to be told that this was not a ferry job but a strike. All the signs were there. Fighting troops not back-ups, good food, cigarettes, and above all an undefined air of tension coming from the Wardroom. Once at sea, we were told our destination was a little place called Anzio, and the intention was to strike straight through to Rome. No pontoons this trip, and we were to have a 'cushy' number this time – they said second wave instead of first. As I've said, we had fighting troops – British 1st Division and Brigade of Commandos with us, and on the morning of January 22nd 1944 we slammed straight into the harbour at Anzio. Alongside an American L.S.T. which had taken the first Wave in, U.S. Rangers under Captain Errol (Flash Alf)[9] Turner R.N. had gone in around 0200 and subdued

---

[9]Extract from 'THE LONDON GAZETTE' Friday 28th July 1944, Tuesday 1st August 1944 to be a Companion of the

what turned out to be weak defences. We came in around 0600 under heavy and continuous shelling and air attacks – 'cushy' the man said?

I had the starboard forward Oerlikon (20mm) and it had plenty of action. With those guns one is strapped in across the back, whilst the shoulders fit into two padded 'horseshoes' to enable a complete traverse simply by moving the feet and firing all the time. The enemy counter-attacked the town but couldn't make it to the dock area. The sun was climbing high to my left when a FW 190 came out of it, straight for us. I could hear it but couldn't see it, so I aimed straight at the sun and gave it everything I'd got. There was a tremendous crash, a rushing of air that emptied my lungs, and a hell of a lot of water. I had no idea what had happened, or where I was, but I knew I should not be thrashing about in water on the upper deck of an L.S.T!

It was about then that I realised I wasn't on an L.S.T., but alongside it, and without conscious thought made frantic swimming motions towards the dock side, which I was now able to make out. Hands grabbed me and dragged me out, and started exploring for holes that shouldn't be there. At least I hoped that was what they were doing, though I couldn't have done much about it right then if it wasn't. Having got my wind back, I discovered that despite being tightly strapped into the gun, I had been blown out and over the side without even a bruise to show for it. (That was not a complaint I might add.) Captain Turner's comment, I was told, was: "If

Distinguished Service Order. Acting Captain Errol Colcannon Lloyd Turner, Royal Navy.

those lads have done swimming, could we have the anti-aircraft guns manned again?"

This L.S.T. landed on the beach at Anzio, although not my ship.

PETER BEACH, ANZIO 22/1/44

Whilst from this photograph, it is difficult to distinguish detail, it does in fact show another 'Party Cable' group unloading from an L.S.T. to the pontoon causeways described earlier. Regrettably, I am not aware of which group it was. As I have mentioned earlier, one rarely knows what's going on outside rifle range and my little lot were being kept quite fully occupied in Anzio Harbour.

Bill Dilworth
51 Chester Rd
Walthamstow
London.E17 7HP.   NOTE NEW TEL No: 020 8520 0235.   Date:31.1.2000.

Dear Anzio Veteran,
                    Enclosed your certificate of Honour presented to you by the citizens of Anzio.
A museum was opened in 1994, the 50th anniversary of the landings and battles of Anzio Beachhead.
I found that there was hardly anything to show of the landings & battle by the British. But plenty to
show of the Italians, Germans & USA. I asked why was this ? and was told that the museum could not
get any help from England.
I stayed with them for five days, introduced members of the museum to the Duke of Kent who was at
the British War Cemetery. And when I left I promised the museum that I would "pull some fingers
out" when I got back to England.
Now nearly 6 years later. I am proud to say the British showing is as great as the others. BUT more
than that, We have also got a great showing for the Royal Navy, which the others have not got.

The Queen mother is pleased with the way things have turned out and is very interested.

Now, Can you help to show more of us British ?. By a photo of you in those days, in uniform ?. to be
shown in the museum. Any maps, documents names & photos of your ship, Regiment, Aircraft.
Memories etc.?.
I shall be returning to Anzio again in the late spring taking anything that comes in, with me.
REMEMBER, WE WERE THERE.

With your Certificate, please put your Regiment, Ship, rank & full name just above the photo. And the
date you get it at the bottom.

I have sent out over 250 so far. We hope you like it. If you know of any Anzio Veteran, please let him
know.   And to those who have asked, THERE IS NO CHARGE for this Certificate. The people of
Anzio feel this is a way to say "thank you Veterans of 1944".

I hope to hear from you one day with any help you may be able to give the museum.

                              Yours sincerly,
                              Bill Dilworth.

CITY OF ANZIO

CERTIFICATE OF HONOUR

TO

THOSE WHO FOUGHT SO VALIANTLY, WITHOUT FEARING FOR THEIR
OWN LIVES, ON THE BEACHHEAD DURING THE BATTLE OF ANZIO

LEST WE FORGET

Peter R.Ellis
Combined Operations LST 424 Seaman Commando LT/JX 425824

ANZIO BEACHHEAD RESEARCH AND DOCUMENTATION CENTER
ANZIO BEACHHEAD MUSEUM

ANZIO **31 JAN 2000**

The President
Patrizio Colantuono

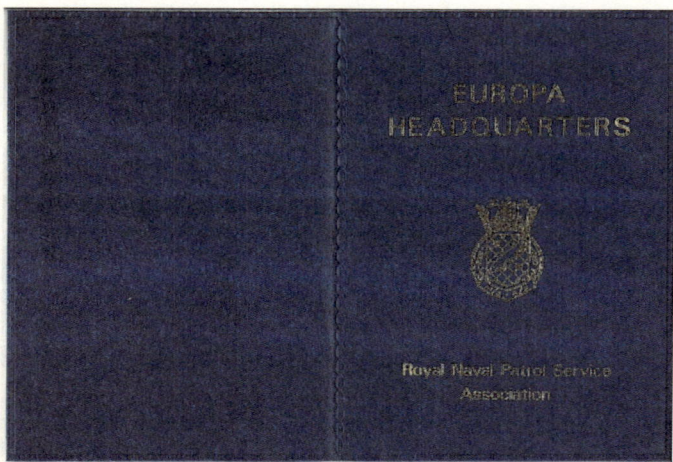

EUROPA
HEADQUARTERS

Royal Naval Patrol Service
Association

I never found out whether my swim was due to the bomb from the FW 190, or a shell from 'Anzio Annie', a railway-mounted gun that trundled out, fired a few rounds, and trundled back again. Neither our planes nor sea fire could nail it as it never stayed still long enough, and did tremendous damage during the first week.

Whilst repairs were made to our bow doors, we did several patrols into the town and down the coast, but only drew sporadic fire.

We were there I think for about a week, during which the shelling never stopped, but the air raids became less frequent and we were not sorry to cast off and head once more for North Africa. German submarines and E-Boats were still very active in the Mediterranean at that time, so there was no let-up in watch-keeping and gun duty.

Before we arrived across the pond, Tubby had sent for me and Gerry Marshall and told us he had made recommendations that we should both be awarded a decoration for our efforts when we had been torpedoed, and sundry other odds and ends. Must have got 'lost in the post' as I never got it! However, what I did get was an approved recommendation to go home and take a commission – when it could be arranged! Knowing the workings of Navy administration systems as, by this time I did, I resigned myself to a long wait.

The next thing of significance to come to mind was a brief respite of a few days at Capri. To relax a little after Anzio they said. Very nice it was too. Peaceful and unspoiled by war, before it was commercialised by the likes of Gracie Fields and her inamorata. The Blue Grotto was shown to us by the local boatmen, and very beautiful it was too. I have never been back, but I understand it's all electric lights and taped music now, and costs a small fortune to see.

We lived on the L.S.T. whilst there, and were tied up alongside H.M.S. Penelope, a 6" Cruiser. H.M.S. 'Pepperpot' she came to be called, presumably because of the amount of damage she took in various actions and still came back fighting. We left on the same day, but she of course could make something like 30 knots, and soon passed out of our sight.

From Capri, we had steamed up the west of Ischia, and then slowly back down the other side to Naples. Naturally, we were dressed in our standard gear of khaki uniforms, with Commando and Combined Operation shoulder flash and Navy caps. No sooner had we gone ashore, amongst all the wreckage that was Naples harbour at that time, than a Master at Arms stepped forward and, to our surprise, said, "All right lads. Take it easy – no need for formality – just go into that warehouse and my lads will fix you up."

The shock of a 'Jaunty' being considerate, even friendly, was almost too much, but one never, ever argued with 'Jaunties' or 'Crushers', so we went into the warehouse. We were sat at long tables, fed magnificently, given a double tot of rum, kitted out with a complete outfit of seaman's gear, including everything we had been issued at training ships, down to a Pusser's dirk (knife), and also a hammock, which Patrol service ratings, mostly, never had.

Falling in outside again, we found Tubby had arrived and taken charge. He was a quick-witted and smart man as I have mentioned. When we disappeared, he quickly found out where we were, and why, and went into action. Pulling rank on the Jaunty he bawled (quite uncharacteristically for him), "Don't mollycoddle these men, get them fell in and looking like sailors, and do it now." To the disgust of our benefactors, he made us do a couple of drill movements, inspected us at attention, and then marched us swiftly and smartly into the city – complete with booty. Once out of sight of the docks, he reverted to his normal self, and explained the situation to us.

It appears that when the Penelope left us. she had run afoul of U 410, and was torpedoed and sunk – (18.2.44). Seeing what appeared to be sailors in army uniforms, the Jaunty, bless his heart, had assumed us to be survivors, and without waiting for confirmation, had treated us as such. Tubby had also followed an old Naval tradition, 'never look a gift horse in the mouth', after all, there was very rarely 'owt for nowt' in the Andrew – or anywhere else for that matter!

We were billeted ashore for a while, and if memory serves, it was in, or very near, Garibaldi Square. Sounds posh, but it wasn't very salubrious.

We had been seconded to help with bringing the docks and harbour area back into full operational use.

This document was issued in December 1943 on my birthday!

Author's note:
Sir John Henry Dacres Cunningham 1885 – 1962

CIC Levant 1943
Allied Naval Commander, Med. 1943-1946
First Sea Lord 1946-1948
Admiral of the Fleet 1948.

Italy was still the scene of bitter fighting, and needed all the supplies delivering as close to our lines as we could manage. The disgraced name of Astor is bitterly remembered by the survivors of that campaign. Disgraced by one woman politician, who referred to the whole of the forces involved in the Italian campaign, as 'D-Day Dodgers' in a speech in Parliament. Where she got the idea that servicemen could choose where they were sent, God only knows. The fact that the woman was totally ignorant, not unusual in politicians, of either the reasons for the campaign, or its part in allowing D-Day 6th June 1944, to take place at all, did little to lessen the bitterness.

Between the bouts of hard work, we managed one or two 'jollies'. Visiting the ruins of Pompeii was one, and this was a trip on the back of a 'Mack'. I always seemed to find those, despite the other makes that abounded. The ruins themselves were shown to us by an old Professor, who had been given the job of caretaker when he no longer had students to teach. His English was fair, and we saw many things that are now, I'm told, kept in air-conditioned and humidity-controlled rooms or cases to preserve them.

Sometime in my travels up and down the Mediterranean, we passed by Etna on Sicily as the volcano was erupting. I am still not sure whether it was Etna or Vesuvius! Even miles out at sea, a rain of fire ash came down on us, and the eruption itself was the most spectacular firework display I have ever seen.

Many things happened which have found no place in this narrative: not from a desire to be selective, so much as memory apparently using its own recall values. I mention this now, since the next thing to come to mind is my severance from Party Cable. Tubby sent for me and told me my recall home had arrived and I would take passage on whatever could be found to take me to Malta.

I got there, but I have no recollection of how. Having reached Malta, I languished for at least six weeks before getting the next passage. I pestered the drafting office every day, and eventually was instructed to join H.M.S. Mauritius which was a Cruiser. I was now what was described in the Andrew, as a C.W. Candidate.

Unknown to me, I had been earmarked as C.W., (Commission and Warrant) potential before leaving Britain. This, of course, I didn't find out until much later.

What I had found out, without understanding the reasons, was that the path of a C.W. rating was far from easy. To attain a commission one had to stand out, to know your job better than your contemporaries, and above all to keep your nose clean!

I had always nurtured the ambition to be an officer and had thus, without knowing that I was being watched, attempted to match and even outdo whatever my immediate companions could do. They, I suspect, were more 'streetwise' than I. At least some of them. With hindsight, I seemed to find more fights out of sight of authority, than even my careful use of correct English would have accounted for. None the less, win or lose, I like to think that bloody nose or not, we were staunch companions when the chips were down. End results, I would suggest, confirm this.

Arriving by tender at the Cruiser, I was given a cabin (small, granted), but unbelievable luxury to me. It must be pointed out here that my position was somewhat unusual in that I was, at that time, a Seaman R.N.P.S travelling in a general service ship. As a C.W. candidate I could not be billeted in with the midshipmen as I was still 'lower deck.' My combined operation status together with the C.W. classification did not allow in KR & AI's for me to be messed with the other lower deck ratings or so my tutor (Lt. R.N. Education – only carried on capital ships of course – who obviously had sea going duties as well) told me at the time. Whatever the reasons it enabled me to brush up on my trigonometry in peace, since I was given no duties aboard the cruiser. I was still wearing khaki, which now had two campaign ribbons, as well as my flashes. I had to report each day for four hours, swotting to refresh my maths for the C.W. course. I distinctly remember the Education Officer, and his help, and also sitting under the 'Walrus' on one of the turrets, to swot as the ship plunged on to wherever it was going.

What, if anything, happened then is a mystery to me. Simply by checking dates in my discharge papers, I have established that something in the order of eight weeks has gone missing from my memory.

I left Malta in April 1944 in the Mauritius. My next memory is approaching the Clyde Estuary in a troopship, no longer in khaki but back in normal seaman's rig. This was late June, and records show I was back on H.M.S. Europa's books at Lowestoft on 1st July, 1944. Someone once said, "We forget because we must, not because we will." I have still no idea whether this is the case with me.

Leave at home was very welcome before I went to King Alfred at Hartley to sit for my commission. Apart from the educational requirements (which presented no problems as, unlike most of my erstwhile comrades I did have a Grammar School education), we did regular assault courses during the weeks I was there. The ones seen these days on 'The Krypton Factor' are a gentle version of the ones we took, but live ammunition as a motivator could hardly be used for television programmes. I recollect four of these courses, one each week, and I took one first, two seconds and a third. This timing suggests I must have been at King Alfred during the D-Day landings at Normandy. I had hoped to have an M.T.B. on my commission to take part in this. My commission was postponed for some time. Due to my foolishly correcting a Commander's French pronunciation whilst we were discussing the "MAQUIS" The actual exchange went something like:

"What do you understand by the 'MackWiss'?"

"Sorry Sir?"

"The French underground man!"

"Oh you mean the 'Mackee'."

"Wait outside!"

I should have known that three ring Commanders serving in their second war, don't take kindly to being corrected by nineteen year old lower deck H.O. ratings!

When I was called back before the selection board – Commodore, 2 Captains, 3 Commanders and a bevy of ADC's who were all Lt. Commanders – I was told that educationally I was acceptable, my experiences in the Mediterranean certainly fitted the qualification requirements but they concluded I was somewhat immature in other respects. Had I anything to say? I had! In retrospect, I proved their point conclusively because I said that I was sure that could be cured by age! The result was commission postponed for 12 months and a further assessment at that time.

Back to Lowestoft and shore based for a spell. I had several odd jobs at this time none of which seems to have been significant enough for me to remember. That is except for the one occasion when I was required to read the lesson on a Sunday Church Parade. I don't know the name of the church we used (this parade was not held in the Sparrow's Nest), but I do recall that we marched there past the Blue Cross club. This, if memory serves, was a sort of 'Aggie Weston's sailors home' type of club based on the Scottish churches.

The best part of being based back in Lowestoft was that we were billeted ashore with the local people. I can only speak, of course, from my own experience but the family I stayed with (I wish I could remember the address) was named Swann and the husband was a member of the Lowestoft Lifeboat crew if not the Coxswain. They were wonderful people and I was never better cared for either before or since.

Later, whilst I was still in the service but after the war was over I was able to take my wife to see Lowestoft and the Sparrow's Nest and we stayed with Mrs Swann. She fed us right royally and when we had fish – it happened to be plaice – it overflowed the large dinner plate in all directions. Another occasion, after a marvellous meal, she asked her husband how he had enjoyed it and he replied, "Gravy's tender gel!" and got chased round the table! Neither my wife nor I have ever forgotten it.

Finding Lowestoft boring and frustrating, I took the only course available at that time: to qualify as an R.P.O. (Regulating Petty Officer). After the work I'd done for my commission, it was no challenge, and I forgot about it. One other thing of note which I recall was playing football in goal for the Navy against the Air Force – local units that was of course. The Air Force team, having been awarded a penalty four minutes from time, with the score at 1-1, were already looking at their next game against the Army. I made my guess at which way to go and dived, and everything came together. The ball hit my fists, went up and over the bar, and we won (on a points system).

I was offered a place in the Navy team, but before I could start a new career, I was drafted to commission a 75ft. M.F.V. This I discovered, stood for Motor Fishing Vessel, and was to be used for many things in the next few months. Timber built, and armed with one Oerlikon, two twin Lewis guns, four rifles and one Smith and Wesson revolver: she was a formidable weapon against the Nazi Navy! Also against our own and anyone else's with the crew we had!

Skipper was an ex-trawler skipper by the name of P.O. Magnus Ingle.

Chief Engineer P.O. Stoker Dickson Jackson.
Second in Command L/Sea. P.R.E. (Roye)
Crew Sea. Bert Farmer
Sea. Jack Dasholt
Sea. H.H. Raymond
Sea. Clucas Crebbin (I.O.M.)

My leading rate came through 27 Jul 1944. I was not informed until sometime later. M.F.V. 1006 was commissioned in Dartmouth, Mac (skipper), and Jock (engineer) brought her to the small craft pool in Portsmouth, where I and the rest joined her.

The following are who I remember of the Charioteers who joined us later for the mine clearance operation in Ostende.

C.O. Lt. H.L.H. Stevens. D.S.C.
Leading Seaman J. Freel. C.G.M.
Leading Seaman A. Ferrier. D.S.M.

Author bottom right.

We did a few working-up runs around the Solent to check that everything worked, and also to size each other up. Mac's old man had owned the 'King Emperor', a trawler out of Leith, and he (Mac) was the best seaman I ever met. What he didn't know about seamanship was never likely to be needed. Jock had worked in Trawlers out of Preston Pans, and could make a diesel engine play 'Annie Laurie' with no discordant notes. The rest of the lads, like me, had come from civilian life, never having seen a ship except on the horizon at Cleethorpes or Blackpool.

I should point out here that Portsmouth was a very different place from when I last saw it. It had been bombed then, but looked so much more battered now. Bombs had demolished entire buildings, and left holes in every street, like gaps in teeth. Air raid shelters and gas decontamination centres were to be found round almost every corner. Kerbstones were painted white, and traffic lights masked. The entrance to all large buildings were sandbagged, and windows criss-crossed with tape. Tanks of water had been placed in the bombed sites. This of course was common to all bombed towns and cities. Most of the changes I saw had been brought about I was told, by V1s (Doodlebugs, Buzz bombs).

Once we had done the 'shake-down' runs, and reported her operational, M.V.F. 1006 became 'Liberty Boat' for anything big that had to lie off in the Solent. My most outstanding memory is of H.M.S. Warspite. (I'd last seen her in the Mediterranean when she was hit by a radio controlled bomb.) We regularly ran Liberty men from the big ships into Portsmouth, and at midnight took them back to the ship before they turned into 'pumpkins'. Or more frequently, liquid matelots.

On one occasion, Mac had issued himself a leave pass and gone home to Edinburgh, and I was acting Skipper. Warspite was in the Solent, and I was signalled to take off her Liberty men at 16:00 hours and return them for midnight. As I approached, the sea was running heavy with a big swell, and, watching the Warspite's blisters (anti-roll devices), I signalled that the only way I could take off the Liberty men was from the Quarterdeck Jacob's ladder.

The Quarterdeck is Officer's country, and anathema for lower deck ratings. In consequence, the deck watch Officer insisted I approached the amidships ladders where the blisters were. I pointed out the dangers; he still insisted! Ours not to reason why. I went in. The sea was not to be denied. As I gently brushed alongside, the Warspite lifted to a swell, and crashing back down stripped fifty of my seventy five feet of freeboard away. I veered away before the next roll to save the rest of my ship. The next signal from Warspite was 'come alongside the Quarterdeck'. This I did, and took off 150 Liberty men, and returned them in a fluid state at midnight when the sea had abated. A message was passed to me to see Commander X on board Warspite at 1300 hours the following day!

Tying up alongside the following day I thought, "You've really blown it this time, don't you ever learn not to tangle with Commanders?" On board amidships, wearing number ones, and saluting like a guardsman, I awaited my Court Martial. The duty Officer, returning my salute said, "Please follow the bosun's mate, the Commander is waiting for you." *I'll bet he is*, I thought.

Just a minute, did he say "please"? This was something outside my knowledge!

Arriving at the Commander's cabin, the bosun's mate announced me and disappeared. What happened next will be hard to believe to anyone with naval experience. The Commander stepped forward, shook my hand, and gave me a drink! He said, "Sorry about yesterday. I had been celebrating my fourth ring and my deck Officer played by the book. Quite rightly, of course. However, my chippies will make good any damage and I shall signal the dockyard that you are under my command temporarily. Meanwhile I shall have your ship provisioned whilst the freeboard is repaired." Apart from saying, "Thank you, Sir." I never said a word and the interview was ended. I even forgot to congratulate him on his promotion. We were loaded with white bread (unseen for God knows how long), hams, sausages and two illicit bottles of whisky immediately, but the repairs were actually carried out in the Dockyard. The strange thing was I never got involved in any paperwork in respect of it and anyone who knows the "Andrew" will appreciate how unusual this was.

The next incident that comes to mind occurred during a return from taking Liberty men back to a Cruiser lying out in the Solent. Once again, I was in charge as Mac was seeing friends in Southsea.

One of our lads, Bert Farmer I think, was going on leave when this trip was over and since he was taking his bottled "Tots" (Rum) home with him, he didn't wish to risk being stopped at the Dockyard gates and searched. This happened randomly since many things tended to disappear in Dockyards. Anyway, I had agreed to cut my riding lights, dim as they were, and drop Bert at the

Railway Jetty which was in fact part of the platform system for the trains. I cut my lights just outside Fort Blockhouse and was immediately challenged by a shore Aldis lamp. Giving the code for the day on our Aldis we were cleared and continued towards the Railway Jetty. (The challenge turned out to be extremely fortunate.) The tide running in either direction at that end of the harbour made coming alongside a very delicate operation. On this occasion, it was ebbing strongly so I had to power past the jetty then turn gently and ease the power to let the tide drift me in so that I was stemming the current and virtually stopped. The concentration on the dim jetty light to judge distance, and having no lights on myself, meant I didn't see the small railway boat tied up where I was about to touch. I certainly heard it, though, as my seventy or eighty tons crushed it against the steel braced jetty.

Bert jumped as planned and disappeared into the darkness, as running feet and loud voices approached to find out what was going on. As the Railway Police arrived I flicked the riding lights back on, and with the loudhailer told them we had lost secondary power and daren't risk running down the harbour without riding lights. I then said power had now been restored, and we were proceeding to the small craft pool, and that a full report would be made on the following morning. There was much shouting but I was already breasting the tide under full power away from there. A full report was made to N.O.I.C.'s office, along the lines indicated, along with an apology to the Railway. This is where the Fort Blockhouse challenge was so useful. The gunnery officer responsible for the harbour entrance cover had rung N.O.I.C. the previous night, about M.F.V. 1006 lurking about without lights, and being lucky not to get blown out of the water. The N.O.I.C.'s office suspected nothing (but I'm not so sure about the Railway Police) and paid for a new boat.

Mac, who was in the habit of signing his own leave passes more frequently than KR's and AI's allowed, took it all very philosophically, although he did wonder out loud how these things always seemed to happen in his absence. He never questioned my boat handling though, because I had conned the ship many times in his presence before he ever let me take her entirely on my own. This was flattering, because as I mentioned earlier, he was a deep sea skipper and a fine seaman. He didn't have much time for spit and polish R.N. discipline, but he expected and received instant obedience to any order once we were on the water. It seems I was lucky once again in my C.O.'s. After the Mediterranean episodes and my involuntary Commando role, M.F.V. 1006 with Mac Ingle was better than any rest camp. All good things come to an end though, and that relaxed lifestyle was no exception. One fine day a signal came aboard saying that in the next few days command of M.F.V. 1006 would be taken over by one Lt. H.L.H. Stevens R.N.V.R. It was obvious we were about to be involved in a different activity, since odd jobs and Liberty men did not warrant a Lieutenant in command unless their Lordships in their wisdom were resting him too. As it turned out that was not so very far off the mark. At least not at first!

Before this happened though I have just remembered another incident. My father, Alick, had designed and patented a marine valve, which when used on the fuel input would, it was believed, give another five knots to the speed of our M.T.B.'s. He had been given the opportunity of testing this belief in an M.T.B. out of Vosper's yard at the bottom end of Portsmouth harbour. When he learned this, I was at that time operating out of Portsmouth, he used his influence with N.O.I.C. and I found myself collected by staff car, in my Number Ones, and being driven round to Vosper's yard. Both Alick and I were treated as V.I.P.'s and taken aboard the M.T.B., in which the valve had already been fitted. No time was wasted in moving out into the English Channel and opening up to full 'chat'. Alick was in the engine room and I was in the main cabin. At full throttle it was an acquired art to stand up, and virtually impossible without something to hang on to.

A previous run had been made with the ordinary valve, and it appeared we had made seven knots better than before, for the same fuel consumption. Unfortunately, I couldn't join in the celebrations, since they were held in the Officers' mess ashore, and I had no civilian clothes. Other ranks were not permitted to drink with Officers in the Wardroom but the sad thing is, that shortly afterwards the patent was rescinded when it was discovered an American had patented the same idea, two days before Alick.

When Lt. Stevens came aboard, we were immediately out of Mac's independent Navy, and back in His Majesty's. Sweaters and woolly hats were out, and uniforms were in. We also took aboard three new crew members and a lot of diving gear, and sundry other tools.

The only name I recall is Jimmy Freel, Palermo C.G.M. (shown on Antiques Road Show, Sunday 8th Nov 1994). Over a period of time, we discovered that these lads, together with Lt. H.L.H. Stevens, had been riding two-man 'chariots' around Norway and Italy, and elsewhere in the Med. Their 'rest' with us, we found, was to seek out mines with the aid of a glass bottom boat and sonic devices, and then dive on them and disable or destroy them. If they found a type not familiar to them, they were to bring it aboard and take it apart to see what made it tick. I have just remembered another name: Alf Ferrier.

On the first leg of our new travels, we sailed to Brixham, and gunnery practice on the way was shooting at a loose mine which was heading inshore on the tide. Having failed either to sink it or explode it on the first pass, we came in for another. I was fortunate enough to be on the Oerlikon. I was unfortunate enough to be just changing pans when whoever was manning the Lewis exploded the mine. We were much too close, and the blast caught the magazine I was loading whilst I only had the back clips in. The result was that I finished up with forty-odd pounds of Oerlikon magazine on my head, more sleepy time, and an enduring headache for over a week. We had no sailing orders so it didn't cause any problems.

The pub on the jetty was called the 'Rising Sun' and had been commandeered by the Navy for use as an administration office. This was where we collected mail, if any, and was always referred to as the 'Japanese Embassy'!

In learning about the dangers of Brixham's secret weapon – "scrumpy" – we had become friendly with the locals, one of whom took some of us to his home, to sample his homemade scrumpy. His furniture was painted with black bitumastic, "to preserve it from the salt air m'dears!" When we spilled some scrumpy on it though, it was, regrettably not able to withstand that. He was quite philosophical about it, and declared that a fresh coat of bitumastic would hide a multitude of sins.

Paint in fact, played quite a part in our Brixham visit. It had been decided by our new Skipper that since M.F.V. 1006 was under new management, so to speak, we ought to paint ship. To the uninitiated, this means chipping or scraping the existing paint off, then 'red-leading' all the surfaces, and then painting either in 'battleship grey', or Mediterranean blue and white. Since the skipper was no slave driver, we worked all morning and had a 'make-do and mend' in the afternoons when we were free to go fishing or whatever else took our fancies. This, for me, was an idyllic couple of weeks, but all good things come to an end.

We were getting fed up with paint, and after sampling Brixham's secret weapon not wisely, but too well one night, it seemed like a hilarious idea to put the statue of William of Orange in his true colours. We hadn't far to go from where we were moored, and the morning saw the famous statue resplendent in red lead. Red lead is, of course, a magnificent orange colour!

Retribution was swift. There didn't seem to be any doubt in the minds of the Mayor and the local constabulary as to who was responsible. Come to that, there didn't seem to be any doubt in the Skipper's mind either. By four o'clock in the afternoon, watched by irate locals, the statue had been scrubbed cleaner than it had ever been seen in living memory, with white spirit and wire scrubbers, and by six o'clock we had received orders to slip harbour and proceed to Ostend the following morning, preferably on the first tide. Pure coincidence I suppose! (This incident has been included in a book which relates the story of the two-man torpedoes, which I once had, but I can no longer remember its title or author unfortunately.)

Ostend was somewhat battered as I remember, but the things that stick in my mind were the nostalgic sounds of piano accordions in little bistro's around the harbour. Masts sticking out of the water everywhere and our divers fetching every sort of mine you could imagine back on board to see if the Skipper could either recognise it or find it in his books. When, as happened often, it was something not documented or experienced, they would sit on the foc'sle with screw drivers, pliers, wire cutters, and note books, and take the bloody thing apart! I used to go and sit on the stern! We were only seventy-five feet long, and if the thing had exploded it would have left no trace of the ship or anyone in it, but it seemed like a good idea at the time. I should point out here that the harbourmaster on these occasions insisted we stood out to sea.

We found the mines by using what was then the most modern technology available: a small ex-landing craft, fitted with a glass bottom, and what must have been a cross between sonar and television. It had a screen which showed a very indistinct picture of the seabed and anything on it. The glass bottom was for inshore shallow water jobs. In either case our divers had to go down and identify what the objects seen might be.

Despite how primitive that approach sounds, we, as a team, became very effective at recognising and eliminating a great many, highly lethal, surprise packages from Ostend harbour. We also found a boat on the seabed which, when we raised it, was found to have a car engine (somewhat modified) to power it. After some days work, Jock was able to clean it all out and get it running, we were then able to examine much of the jetty structure, and found several more explosive little presents. We also used it for our own pleasure, until someone pulled rank on our Skipper and we lost it.

That, incidentally, was where I learned to 'scull' a boat with one oar. Having run out of petrol (as I said, it had been a car engine) at the wrong side of the harbour, I remembered the boats in Valletta (Malta). These boats were propelled by using one oar from stern, and twisting it in a figure of eight. After a few experiments, it suddenly all came together and we got back to our own side of the harbour in relative comfort. Moreover, we still had the boat, which we certainly would not have had were it to be left unattended whilst we 'searched' for petrol.

Once cleared for shipping, Ostend became a staging point (one of several) for troops reinforcing the advance on Germany as well as for repatriated troops the other way. One day, it came to my attention that the 23rd. Field Co. R.E's were in the transit camp just on the outskirts. My brother, Arthur, had served with them, supporting the 8th Army in the North African desert. (I learned after the war that he had discovered my resting in Tripoli by some chatter from our L.R.D.G. friends, and made his way there, only to see me sailing into the distance.) Skipper raised no objection to my checking out the camp to see if Arthur was still with the same outfit. I hitched a lift to the camp but, like all transit camps, its function was to pass people through to wherever they were ordered, as quickly and efficiently as possible. In consequence, the clerks handled so many thousands of people, from so many different units, that remembering individuals was not a viable bet. I talked to R.E's from whatever companies I could find, but had no success.

Two days later we were ordered to Falmouth. Our job was finished at Ostend, and others had taken care of other ports, so we were to be decommissioned. Again, only after the war did I find that my enquiries had reached Arthur eventually and he had, without benefit of permission, taken a truck from the pool and come straight down to the harbour. Once again when he enquired for M.F.V. 1008, he was informed that the small vessel just clearing the boom defence was 1006 on her way to Blighty!

As it turned out we had also narrowly missed each other in Italy too.

We decommissioned at Falmouth, and I was sent back to Lowestoft. I learned at this time that I had passed out, top of the course for my R.P.O. rate. However, before I could be kitted out in P.O's fore and aft rig, I was posted to H.M.S. Clover, K134 (Flower class Corvette as described in 'The Cruel Sea'.) late November 1945 at Campbeltown, which was commanded by one Tom Fanshawe, who I was to meet many years later in connection with the Sea Cadets.

Almost my first action on entering the mess deck was to step between two seamen who were about to knock seven bells out of each other. I told them I had no objection to them killing each other, providing they did it on the jetty, and not on my mess deck. I was at this time, still a 'Killick' – Leading Seaman – and had been given that particular mess. With what I found out later, I would not have been so eager to step between them. After I left the ship, one killed the other with a knife, and I, by a

100

strange coincidence, had the killer in cells at Lowestoft when my R.P.O. promotion had fetched me back there.

Before that though, we did many runs down through the Irish Sea, and round the Isle of Man. Indeed, although I was only aboard the Clover for a short time, we spent some time in the North Atlantic, and that, in winter, on a Corvette, is not a pleasant way to cruise. The most dangerous part of my stay aboard her was when I was designated as 'buoy jumper'. We would often tie up to a buoy in the Channel, rather than alongside, and someone had to jump to the buoy to shackle on the cable. In a force eight, and wearing wet and heavy oilskins and sea boots, this was no easy task, and scared the hell out of me. One slip from a bouncing buoy wearing that gear would have left total reliance on the lifejacket, and I had no faith it could support all that weight. Fortunately, I never had to find out.

Posted back to Lowestoft at the beginning of February 1946, I took up my R.P.O. rate, and became a 'barrack stanchion' for a while. I didn't much care for that. The war had ended with the Germans surrendering on the 8th May 1945, and the Japanese on the 14th August 1945, after atomic bombs had been dropped on Hiroshima on the 6th August 1945, and Nagasaki on the 9th August 1945. (The Carrying plane was 'Enola Gay'.)

Offers were made to me to take a special course, after which I would pick up my suspended commission, and be answerable to some mysterious section based at the Admiralty in Whitehall. The offers came from both Naval Officers and civilians (although I felt they held service ranks), and some pressure was brought to bear inasmuch as they clearly knew all about me and my service record, but would not give the slightest hint of what was expected from me. All I could discover was that once I had re-signed the Official Secrets Act (I had signed in Sousse without really knowing why), they could tell me more. Incidentally, I had always thought that once signed, the Official Secrets Act was for life. It appears that the particular form I had signed in Sousse, related only to the period of hostilities.

Anyway, after a lot of thought, I declined the offers, and was posted to Hoo Camp in Chatham to await my demob.

This eventually arrived on August 17th 1946.

To my surprise, but with much relief, I had made it through the war and was slung back to the real world, holding a firm conviction that I would never volunteer for anything again, and a handful of campaign medals.

War is hell. Peace will kill you!

1939 – 45 STAR
ATLANTIC STAR
AFRICA STAR
ITALY STAR
DEFENCE MEDAL
VICTORY MEDAL
BATTLE FOR BRITAIN
GENERAL SERVICE CROSS
VOLUNTEERS MEDAL

Most of the medals, you will note from the photograph, were not presented until after the war.

Preface to the Island

Realising, a little belatedly, that the events I write about belong to my generation but not necessarily to that of the reader, I have added a little background information.

Maybe some of you reading this remember the earlier writing. If so perhaps you could be curious enough to continue reading. Stranger things have happened!

In April 1942, the British were losing badly and the Americans were still smarting over Pearl Harbour (you are, no doubt, aware that a high proportion of Americans are of German origin and had half expected to enter the war on Hitler's side). In fact, many actually lobbied their senators to pursue that course and the Russians were in a hell of a mess!

It was, as has undoubtedly been said, Hitler's finest hour!

His opportunist allies, the Japanese weren't doing too badly either. They had just conquered an Empire that stretched from the boundaries of India to within striking distance of Australia inside three months and at almost no cost to themselves. They took Hong Kong in December, Malaya in January and Singapore in February. Singapore was, needless to say, the biggest single surrender in British military history. They also sank "Prince of Wales" battleship, "Repulse" a battlecruiser and destroyed an Anglo-Dutch fleet.

This was certainly not good for prestige!

We, the British, were still trying to repair the badly dented pride from 1941 when we had failed to save Greece, almost another Dunkirk, then failed to hold Crete!

Command of the Mediterranean had been lost. Italian frogmen had sunk two battleships in Alexandria Harbour and German U-boats sank the aircraft carrier "Ark Royal" and the battleship "Barham". Malta was, of course, under daily siege by the Luftwaffe.

All this was to change though. At the end of 1942 I took a hand in events! Boastful? Certainly. The impact of my involvement has never, to my knowledge, been recorded anywhere. In order to verify the events in which I took part, I attempted to research the Admiralty records. Apart from one brief but appreciative mention by the then C in C. Mediterranean, who seemed to be under the impression we were a dockyard recovery group, I found no mention whatsoever of the numerous clandestine operations we were involved in. Where decorations had been awarded the "Gazette" statements of why were so vague as to give no clues.

In this day and age, when patriotism seems to be a dirty word, at least as far as the Brussels "idiots" are concerned (they regard it as racist and not "politically correct"), I suppose most people, if they believed this account at all, would choose to think it was some fabrication more akin to the febrile imagination of film producers than a factual account.

Now I have decided to add this last remembered skirmish I will leave it to whoever may read it to make up their own mind. I have no interest in how they do this or in any conclusions they may make. I know what events I took part in and, for me, there is no other truth than that.

The impression I attempted to give about my own impact on the factual situations evolving at the time was, as I am quite sure you understood, purely facetious.

The truth I have just mentioned is that I was caught up with neither inclination nor intention in situations over which I had no control and, I might add even less enthusiasm for! A very different attitude, very rapidly discovered, from that I had been foolish enough to volunteer with.

The following incident did not seep through into my memory until long after the earlier part was written although odd bits of it had done. Usually in what I suppose were dreams, or perhaps more correctly nightmares!

The Island

My last clandestine job, or more correctly, the last one I can remember, was a non-attributable operation. That is – "If you're taken, we do not know you!"

I was part of an S.S.R.F. (Small Scale Raiding Force) and the action was among the Greek Islands. I never knew which one (this was always on a 'need to know' basis), so I couldn't identify it even if I went looking for it!

Having made three landings on enemy held beaches and an abortive submarine operation, I have to admit, in honest vernacular, to being shit-scared beforehand on all of them. People who have known me in later years have found it difficult to believe I did these things. I don't blame them. What they choose to believe is their problem not mine and sometimes I find it difficult myself to realise the extremes to which I went in the overriding instinct for survival in those far off days.

When it came to this operation – unanticipated, not in the known plan, defences down in the belief of a peaceful (so far as any sea voyage could be in those days) trip home to take a Commission – my mind was suddenly overtaken by a small voice telling me; "No way! You can't lose on this one – You'll probably trip over the dog and fall downstairs to get yours but not this little jolly with these boys! The S.B.S. (Special Boat Service) have been there and done it before!" They had too! But I had also done some equally hazardous and similar things. Strangely, what worried me most was the fact that I had never had a dog!

It did cross my mind to wonder why I was ordered on an unmistakeable S.B.S. operation. I suppose all Special Forces come under the same umbrella to the "planners!" With hindsight, I concluded it was something to do with going home for a commission. Some sort of test. In fact, it was more likely that, since I had been shuttled around from one situation to another for the whole of my Mediterranean posting, I was just a number and did as I was told. I'd done little else since I joined! A destroyer took us to a position a few miles from the Island and the Gemini's were launched. These were rigid rubber boats, air-filled and powered by very powerful and singularly quiet outboard motors. I always wanted to have a go at driving those but regrettably never got the chance! The landing itself, although they were all nerve-wracking was quiet, thankfully. We ghosted up to the beach and crept up to the scrub line listening for any sounds that might have meant we were observed. Nothing in the area gave any indication that we had been seen. The Greeks, we were told, were very anti-German. Unfortunately, we were also told they were not particularly pro-British so we had no idea which way they would react. It must have been April 1944, I think, and the ground was hard and rocky. Some cover was provided by the rocks and straggly bushes but what light there was kept disappearing behind clouds. This was something I knew all about. As a boy, camping, I had crept within 10 feet of my friends in the woods without their knowledge until I let them know. Not always appreciated!

Our main objective was a small radio outfit which relayed any and all information being passed by whatever they could eavesdrop on. Ship movements, aircraft directions, in fact any military movements. Insignificant really! Once started on any mission, all concentration was on completion and survival so we never thought during the operation about irrelevant things like "Why or what's the point when a light bomber could take the place out with practically no risk?" However, it rapidly went wrong! I would guess half a mile or thereabouts from the target we were fired on. Duggie Pomford (big guy, fought Bruce Woodcock British Heavyweight Champion, either early in or before the War started) was on my left and Paddy Webster was on my right. His job was to blow up the radio unit. As it happens it was blown up by the R.A.F. later. I suppose by now you are wondering why we were there at all. You may be surprised to learn that it was quite a long time afterwards that that thought occurred to me! Sorry to disappoint you but I never did discover the answer to that one! Someone somewhere knew why but I never did. To say it was a shock would be a massive understatement. I have no idea by whom or what the attack was made. Not that it made any difference at that point in time! The whole German garrison was alerted. I don't think there were many of them but certainly a lot more than there was of us. With surprise gone, we had no choice but to fall back and get the hell out of there. If we could! It became 'shoot where you thought it was coming from' whilst your wing man ran back; he dropped to the ground and gave covering fire whilst you ran back. This all the way back to the beach and it seemed a hell of a lot further going back than it had coming and that had seemed long enough. If they had got behind us, between us and the beach, we were done for. Luck held out for most of us and only two failed to reach the water. I'm ashamed, now, to admit my only concern was that I was not one of those two. I have no idea if they survived or not.

It was still quite dark and we could not have been far in front of the enemy but they were not anxious to get too close since we were firing at flashes apparently with some success. With gut-wrenching relief, we saw the water in the bay cream as the launches swept in. Magazines were emptied at the scrub line to keep their heads down and we dashed into the surf waist high, cursing as the water slowed us down. Support fire was now coming from the launches but they had to be careful to avoid hitting us. Strong arms grabbed anything they could reach and we were dragged inboard and dumped unceremoniously in the scuppers. This, I hasten to add, is definitely not a complaint!

Having been rescued by S.B.S. from this very uncomfortable situation, we were given mugs of strong, sweet tea laced with rum as the launches powered away out to sea. Nothing, I thought, had ever tasted so good or so strong!

After the first sip, I murmured, "Just one cousin in Ollerton apart from family!"

"What the hell does that mean?" growled the Commander.

"Next of kin," I said.

"Cheeky sod," he muttered.

He must have thought I was referring to the way he

was hurling the launch from wave crest to wave crest and hitting them with a bone-juddering thump and with apparent abandon. He could have been right but I was only too happy to be able to feel it and it was really much more to do with the fusillade coming from the shore line. To be fair there was certainly nothing reckless in his boat-handling he had done this sort of thing many times.

Anti-climax, a nervous twitch and, I suppose, the rum made the rest of the trip hazy for me. I vaguely remember transferring to something bigger which I guess would be the Destroyer that had delivered us and later to what I have to assume was the Mauritius because I certainly can't remember. I didn't really care at that time.

From there on nothing has surfaced in memory which is probably just as well! I just don't know.

It's taken fifty plus years for this one to seep through and I don't think I want to know if there are any more! This brief note of one of my activities during the war was finally written in the second Millennium but what was left of my old notebooks and scraps of paper from many years ago showed where flashes of memory which eventually penetrated can be related to things that were, but perhaps shouldn't have been written down without fully revealing the incident.

Rightly or wrongly, they have now been eliminated but, more importantly, they gave no clue as to why the task was undertaken in the first place. It was clearly known that information was being passed from that area and it was equally obvious that a Beaufighter could have taken the radio out with practically no risk. We had almost complete air superiority then. Always supposing I have identified the right point in time to place it!

These thoughts didn't occur to me until long afterwards when I had some bad nights thinking of the guys who didn't come back. Someone somewhere knew why it happened but that sort of information seldom, if ever, gets to the sharp end except in books written by uninvolved people. In any event one did not question orders from people in superior positions to one's own—at least until one had much more clout than a bottom of the heap, expendable Commando!

I do think the island job must have taken place in the blank period for which, previously, I had no recall. The glimpses of memory leave many questions unanswered. When, for example, did I get together with my colleagues on the job and where? Every operation I took part in was trained for separately so where did we train for this one? Who was commanding the operation? How many Gemini's did we use?' Perhaps it's better not to know any more answers!

I can recall some names although, initially, I did not know where they fitted or how I knew them.

Duggie Pomford I have already mentioned.

Paddy Webster I associate with explosives I have also mentioned.

Names I still can't fit are Billy Reeves, Ray Jones, Syd Greaves, Maurice Pound, Halibone and Wildgoose. Please bear in mind that, although we must have been together long enough to know who was who and what part each of us would play, I had also lived for three months in close proximity with thirty or so others in basic training and few of those names remain with me either.

When I first started writing these memories in 1990, I planned to leave out many of the incidents which occurred that I believed were not the sort of things that my grandchildren, or for that matter, any of my family should know about. Now, in 2004, I still believe that was not wrong. Regrettably I also realize that the Island incident, relatively sanitized as it is, should never have been started. A cohesive whole story of the action is not possible with so many gaps of memory. What has come back may or may not account for the blank period. I no longer want to know!

VE 8/5/45   *VJ 15/8/45*

When I remember all
The friends so linked together
I've seen around me fall,
Like leaves in wintry weather
I feel like one
Who treads alone
Some banquet hall deserted
Whose lights are fled
Whose garlands dead
And all but he departed.

Thomas Moore

Glossary
Abbreviations

A.B. Able Bodied (Seaman)

Bofors 40mm Cannons. Usually anti-aircraft

Brownings Machine Guns

C.G.M. Conspicuous Gallantry Medal

C.O. Commanding Officer

C.P.O. Chief Petty Officer

CRUSHER Regulating Petty Officer

D.C.M. Distinguished Conduct Medal (Non-commissioned personnel)

D.S.C. Distinguished Service Cross (As D.C.M. but for commissioned ranks)

D.U.K.W. Amphibious landing craft

HE Heads High Explosive Heads

HO's Hostility only ratings

JAUNTY Master at Arms

JU88 Junkers dive bomber

K Rations Small one day ration packs

MACK 10 ton American lorry

M/C Machine Gun

M.P. Military Police

M.T.B. Motor Torpedo Boat

N.A.A.F.I. Canteen Service (Navy, Army, Air Force

Institution)
Oerlikons 20mm Machine Cannons
O.S.S. Office of Strategic Services
P.T.I. Physical Training Instructor
R.A.F. Royal Air Force
R.E. Royal Engineers
R.E.M.E. Royal Electrical & Mechanical Engineers
R.P.O. Regulating Petty Officer
S.O.E. Special Operation Executive
Spandau German machine-gun
Stuka Junkers's 87B Dive bomber
Thompson Sub-machine guns
'WALRUS' Flying boat with Pusher engine. Wheels too.

Sir I admit your general rule
That every Poet is a fool
But you yourself may serve to show it
That every fool is not a Poet!

Samuel T. Coleridge.

Poetry

Unless otherwise attributed, everything in this book is
original Roye.

The Lemon Grove (Sicily)

My first Beach-head Assault.

Beneath these trees we lie and dream,
Of things gone by now dimly seen,
As shadows of the things we knew,
'Neath other skies not quite so blue;

Yet clearer to our memory's eye,
These dreams grow, as with homesick sigh,
We search the clear Sicilian sky,
With many a long and piercing look,
Just listening to a rippling brook,
And trying to place the foliage there,
In English meadows, green and fair.

Then suddenly this dream is slain,
As from those snowy clouds again,
Swoops down in rocketing descent,
A winged death, fain to relent,
Until from plain, and beach and hills,
A hail of leaden fury stills,
All life, and leaves this hurtling shell,
To make its own eventual Hell!

I still have the original tatty scrap of paper on which this was written in a lemon grove just south of the beach near Floridia where I landed in 1943. Please bear in mind I was only 18 at the time.

Salerno

My second beach landing and the worst!

The golden sands of Italy ran red with British blood,
As man by man they wilted down in the hail of shell
flung mud,
The German troops were fighting hard, surprise was on
their side,
But slowly we had thinned their ranks and one by one
they died.

Our assault was weakened too, our backs against the
wall,
We'd gained two hundred yards of beach but the group
was getting small.

Tobacco and tomato plants in rich profusion grew,
How many men lay dying there the good Lord only
knew.
The fertile soil of Italy with British blood was fed,
The living ranks were digging in beside the silent dead.

Foot by foot and yard by yard we forced the Nazis back,
Each yard we gained was like a wedge in an ever

widening crack.
By dawn we'd driven three miles in,
The fight was bitter still,
When suddenly the Panzers charged straight down the
bloody hill.

No infantry could then advance against such heavy odds,
Our harried group was fighting hard, we lost belief in
Gods.
The beach was held at enormous cost,
The advance could now go on,
The price was paid by those who lost,
The pain by those who won!

*This again, is from the original scraps written in
gaps of the fighting. For this reason plus the fact that I
was still only 19 years old, the loss of faith is, I hope,
understandable.*

*The final lines refer to the fact that those of us who
survived could never understand why we did and others
didn't. Winning at that cost left a pain that has never
disappeared.*

One of My Landings

A silvery moon bestowed its light o'er sandy shore,
As slowly, silently we nosed our way to land,
The sea, relaxed and still, could not have helped us
more,
Our strength was freedom and our Maker's hand.

But light spelt danger to this bold attempt of ours,
To rip aside aggression's filthy shroud.
So we approaching, prayed throughout the hours,
For zero hour to fall beneath a cloud.

It came; our prayers had not been made in vain,
With softly grating jar we beached at last,
On alien enemy soil we must retain,
And then that hot and withering leaden blast!

*This one was written in a lull and I suspect, although
I can't remember, that it also referred to Salerno. I'm
sure there was more of it now lost but one thing is
abundantly clear. I obviously had not lost all my faith at
that time.*

Friend

Sometimes he'll come in the middle,
Sometimes it's nearer the end,
To some he will bring fear and terror,
But on one thing you'd better depend,
Although you may think he's in error,
Though his word you may never have heard,
He never yet missed an appointment,
Nor ever has broken his word.
The first time I knew he was near me,
I was lying face down in the sand,
The one he'd just taken had tripped me,
His blood was all over my hand.

A soft whispered voice drifted over my ears,
Quite clear despite bombs, guns and shells,
"Not you this time in fact not for years,
But there'll be neither warning nor bells.
I'll tell you today that what I intend-
And you know that my promise is kept-
When I come for you, as you know that I must,
I shall finally come as a friend.

We met several times in the fighting,
His message was always the same,
Not that I actually saw him,
Just a whisper, a flicker, a flame,
His words were not loud or demanding,
"Just get on with life while you can,
For no one may stand where you're standing,
When I come I shall take the right man.

We met yet again sometime later,
On a Dante-like factory floor,
The carbon monoxide had seeped from the hole,
And I looked once again through his door.
"Not your turn yet", he said once again,
There was nothing at all to be seen,
Until the Oxy-mask lifted, my heavy eyes opened in
pain,
It passed as it does and the years drifted by,
Then one day I felt nearly dead,
I discovered through slow focused, struggling eye,
I was flat on a Hospital bed.

I've not had a visit since that one,
Though sometimes I feel he's been near,
But living on time that's been borrowed
You don't seem to feel as much fear.
More often you think you can hear him,
And you guess that you're reaching the end,
When you finally actually see him,
You'll recall what he told you to start with,
He is coming to you as a Friend.

Another close brush with the reaper,
My heart now feeling the strain,
An ambulance dash with the medics,
They make it in time once again.
As I lay with electrodes and dials,
I felt that my friend was quite near,
But the nurses hard heels on the floorboards,
Was all that impinged on my ear.
Now I knew that I'd not yet been sent for,
His way is not that of a sneak,
When he does come for me, out of friendship,
He'll do me the honour to speak.

Poetry is not something learned at school, from a book
or a monastery cell,
It comes from the heart, from the head, from the mind
and from where else whoever can tell.

If you think of the best things you've known, that you've
seen, that you've felt,
Then write it all down just the way that it comes-I forgot
and the way that it smelt;

You'll maybe remember when you see it that way,
All the beauty, the love and the dreams,
The sunshine the rain, the flowers the grass,
The sea and the fields and the streams;

But maybe for you it's not like that at all,
Maybe for you it's all grey,
And the soft summer breeze and the warm golden sands,
Don't send your mind soaring away.

I'm sorry if that's how you find it,
I know there's too much that is bad,
But the best things are there if you seek them,
You can find them and cease to be sad.

Take What Today Has to Offer

Yesterday has gone and tomorrow's yet to come.

The past is a well-read story,
The future an unopened book,
The present is still unfolding,
And it's not all directed by luck.

Some will adapt to whatever,
To things they know they can't alter,
Others will lose what's still there in life,
For they'll weep and they'll groan and they'll falter.

They'll miss the few good things around them,
For wanting to change what they've got,
While the ones who adapt to whatever,
Find that life can still offer a lot,
So don't wish for things you have not,
Make the best of whatever you've got.

Laugh at the rain and the sunshine,
And take it whatever they send,
For it won't make a damned bit of difference,
When your plug is pulled out at the end!

*I don't remember when this was written but it's
fairly clear I had been feeling sorry for myself and then
realized how lucky I really was!*

Unexpected

The most unexpected of days,
You think your tomorrows have gone,
You lie in a pain ridden haze,
And your mind wanders on and on.

People glide in and out of your sight,
Your body won't do as it's told.
It's daytime or maybe it's night,
All you know is you're feeling the cold.

<u>ALL</u> my family have been here before,
They know how it feels to be limp,
So I'll shut up and not be a bore,
Or I'll risk being the family wimp!

Roye, June 1999, Rotherham General Hospital

Childhood

My childhood was never boring,
I learned about flowers and trees,
I watched joyous skylarks soaring,
And something of birds and the bees,
Water instinctively drawing,
Fish making mystical swirls,
If it hadn't have been for this goddamned war,
I might have learned something of girls!

Another wartime one written on the back of an
envelope.

The Test

I've sailed on a number of oceans
And I've fought on a number of shores,
I've met a great number of morons,
And more than my fair share of bores.

That's par for the course I imagine,
No one said that life had to be fair,
I'm sure it's the same for most others
Though I've never been one to compare.

Some people just have to feel better
By being 'one up' on the rest,
But the ones that I feel most at home with,
Are the ones who stand up to the test.

And what is the test? You will ask me,
If you don't I'll be very upset,
It's the fact that the people you're seeing,
Are the same as they were when first met!

July 2000

The Last Leaf on the Tree

It's Christmas and the leaves have dropped;
All, that is but one,
The wind has howled and the rain has poured
And the floods have favoured none.

With all of that I find it sad,
Don't know if it's just me?
To look out from my window,
At the last leaf on the tree.

But it cheers me when I look across
To the tree on the other side,
Beneath which thrusts a snowdrop
In its lonely, lovely pride.

I have a host of snowdrops, back and front, but just the one that comes through before the rest and flowers right into the New Year when the others show themselves.

December 2000

No One Lives Forever

No one lives forever,
At least that's what I'm told,
I don't know who would want to,
It's no fun being old,
Arthritis in the fingers,
And I always seem to find,
I'm moving much too slowly,
For impatient folk behind.
But don't think this is just a moan,
It certainly is not,
I'm lucky not to be alone
And I'm happy with my lot.
My garden's full of flowers,
My grass is fresh and green,
The bulbs will come again in spring
Just as lovely as they've been
And beauty's all around you when you hear the wild
birds sing.

Don't worry on how long you've got,
It's nothing you can alter,
Take life and just enjoy the lot,
One day your steps <u>will</u> falter
And when they do there's no regrets,
You've had a bonus life,
For you've bounced back from all upsets
To reach the end of strife.

Roye, December 2001

Seasons

The apples have gone from the trees,
The Martins and Swallows have flown,
There's no sign of wasps or of bees,
And the roses are drooping and blown,

Summer is certainly over,
Autumn is all red and gold,
There's still a few whispers of clover,
But the air is already quite cold.

Roye, September 2001

Islands

And so we've had another day
Of poetry and prose,
And each of us will be alone
When the day draws to a close,
If you wake up in the morning
When the day is cold and raw,
And you know somebody loves you
You will be alone no more.

Roye, February 2002

Summer

The bees are busily counting flowers,
The birds are checking trees,
The hoverflies are hovering still regardless of the
breeze,
The garden's in full bloom just now,
And the weeds are growing too,
The grass grows more with every shower
And there's always more to do.
But this time of year is full of sights
To delight the eyes of man,
So I'm not too keen on the fall of nights
To take them away again.

Roye, Peter, August 2001

Age

All the bits are wearing much faster than I thought,
It seems that youth's excesses are very dearly bought,
The currency of youth, of course, is energy and zest,
I wish someone had told me it was wiser to invest!
But nothing ever changes and the lesson's only learned,
When we realize we should have crossed the bridges that
we burned.

Roye, January 2002

Celebrate, Don't Mourn

I've lived and I've loved and I think it's fair that the
reaper should hang round my door,
He's left me alone for my three score and ten and also
for quite a few more,
So if he decides that enough is enough you will certainly
not hear me whine.
For he's left me alone whilst my peers have all gone and
I think he's treated me fine,
So when he collects me as we all know he will, don't
mourn that I'm no longer here,
Just remember the times that we've shared in the past
and let's all have just one more beer.

Another year has slipped away.
I wonder where they go.
And why does time get oh so fast,
Whilst we get oh so slow?

Roye, January 2002

Times Change, Honour Is Constant

You've never done the things I've done,
You've never been where I have been,
You'll never see what I have seen,
But friend do not despair,
I'll never do what you will do,
I'll never go where you will go,
I'll never see what you will see,
But who thinks life is fair?
You'll find we sometimes walk in fear,
Sometimes we walk in love,
You'll find we walk alone as well,
But friends are always near,
Don't show enemies you hurt,
Stay on the path you've chosen,
Your honour is your spoken word,
Their broken words are dirt.

Roye, December 2001

Don't Worry, I'm Not As Bitter
As You May Think!

I'll be called to account for the men that I've killed,
And I don't really have a defence,
For who can accept the taking of life,
When no war has ever made sense?
We think we're protecting a way of life,
We think we're protecting our friends,
It's not till we're old that we realize,
It's all for Political ends!
Some think I'm cynical in my views,
My friends and my dearest ones all,
But they haven't run up an enemy beach,
And watched as the dying fall.
Young and stupid, just like me,
Who thought it was honour we served,
And only now do we start to know
THEY never got what they deserved!

Roye, July 2002

Friendship

I know I am out of my depth,
I can't accept all modern trends,
Foes are too easy to make,
It's never so easy with friends.
I'm lucky with what I have got,
Who chooses who I don't know,
With good ones you don't need a lot,
With friendship you must let it grow,
So when you see it first sprout,
Feed it well like a plant or a flower,
If you can, replace all you take out,
It repays you with each passing hour.

Roye, July 2002

Dreams

Dreams are mysterious things
One visits impossible worlds
We fly though we've never had wings
And the structure of time gets unfurled
On falling the fear is so real
No damage is there when we rise
We don't even question the feel
And we wake with but little surprise
All the rules have returned with a start
Now that gravity's once more the norm
The beat has slowed down in your heart
And life's back to familiar form
Sometimes we would like to hang on
To that life which we know is not ours
But the things that we love would be gone

No more birds, no more trees, no more flowers
So enjoy dream's escape whilst you can
But don't let them lead you astray
Choose your own way to follow the plan
Or you'll simply, like mist, drift away.

Roye, September 2002

147

Autumn

The summer has not quite finished yet
We are still getting warm, lovely days
Morning's grass is all dewy and wet
And we wake to a light, misty haze

But days now are shorter and gold
The sun's low as it drifts to the west
The evenings are getting quite cold
The young Martins have all left the nest

They need to stoke up for the long journey south
With insects they take on the wing
It's well known for sure strength goes in at the mouth
Do you know if a Martin can sing?

I hope they'll come back in the spring
When the trees and the flowers are in bud
I couldn't care less if they sing
Just to see them again would be good!

Roye, September 2002

Mirrors

I know that they think I'm old fashioned,
I'm happy to have it that way,
Each age has its own set of values,
Mine certainly aren't of today.

The media devalues the language,
They take all the worst from the Yanks,
Who speak un-grammatical rubbish,
And glorify gangsters and cranks.

But I'd hate to have left the impression,
All the wrong things are over the sea,
The values that I think are better,
Are just a reflection of me!

Roye, September 2002

Scarborough Warning

I've just had a Scarborough warning,
If you know what that means you're O.K.
If you don't I can very soon tell you,
Then you'll know what it means on YOUR day.

It says you've gone over the limit,
Whatever that limit may be,
I assure you, you'll know that you've done it,
For the outcome you just wait and see.

I've had lots of friends who've gone past it,
They aren't here to tell me the score,
If there is a world there, through the exit,
They'd have been back to tell me before.

So square up to life and enjoy it,
Let's face it we aren't here for long,
Don't look for a maybe? Tomorrow?
For today you are <u>here</u>, you <u>belong</u>!

Roye, October 2002

To Gail and Colin

You've read our views on friendship,
We're sure it's overdue,
To practice what we're preaching,
And substantiate the view,
We hope this won't offend you.
That's the last thing we require.
Just think of us occasionally,
When you look towards the fire.

MERRY CHRISTMAS
AND HAPPY BIRTHDAYS.

Love from Iris and Peter.

I sought the verse
I sought the phrase
To tell you how I feel
I never found the magic words
But this, at least, is real.

I used to look at eyes of blue and dream they'd be
forever true,
And then I found two eyes of grey and thought they'd be
there every day,
Until I met those eyes of green with depths that I had
never seen,
And then I found those eyes of brown and knew I'd seek
no more.

Wondering

Perhaps I'll be remembered for what I've left behind,
I'm sure it's much more likely that I'll not,
You can guarantee that's one thing that won't be on my
mind,
For by then a mind is what I haven't got!
The mark we make in this life is what other people
know,
While ever they remember we will never, ever go,
But who will ever know us when contemporaries are
gone?
The answer, if we've left no mark, is very simply-
NONE!

Roye, the last day of 2002

The Death of a Friend

It's not enough, I must complain,
A few lines in the press.
To mark a life that's over now
Of hopes and joys and pain.

Of service in a time of war
Where many more did not
And bringing up a family
For whom her dreams were more.

If only we could pass along the contents of our brain,
The sights the sounds, the things we know,
Experience uniquely bought,
Was all this life in vain?

Who celebrates our time on earth?
How many, by next year,
Will think of things we've done or said
Is this all that we're worth?

I think, perhaps, we want or need
Belief from those who care
That our time here has been worthwhile,
At least in hope and deed!

On the death of Elsie Bilston, Roye, 14th March 2003
Stanley Patrick Bilston died in November of the same
year.
He, like me, was an ex-Beachhead Commando.

Nightmares

I've done what it takes
And I know what it makes,
I thought they were right to ask!
But I'm old now and know what it cost me,
An immoral, unjustified task.

I did it and thought I was chosen,
It all seemed so clear to me then.
The true values must have been frozen
And I've never slept easy again!

I did what I did,
I am what I am,
I ask no forgiveness for this,
But if I could undo it,
And live my own life
Some parts of my past I would miss!

Roye, August 2003

156

Changes

The Martins all have flown this week,
To warmer climes than ours,
The leaves are falling from the trees,
The petals from the flowers.

Those little birds so small and sleek,
Fly south so far away,
Three thousand miles at least they go,
But they'll be back some day.

The mists and frosts are with us now,
Short days and nights are long,
Winter's knocking at the door,
And few birds are in song.

But autumn has its beauty too,
Not everything is bleak,
The golden, russet trees and shrubs
Are never hard to seek.

I'm always looking forward,
To each season's different shifts,
They all have much to offer,
With their individual gifts.

Roye, September 2003

Welney

The fishing and the evening light,
The pub, the stories and the food,
The ones you've caught the ones you might,
The crackle of the burning wood.

Sometimes the cards would last till late,
The moon on outside toilets shone,
Who won, who lost was left to fate,
To end the game no harm was done.

The morning's breakfast full of fat,
Prepared us for the day to come,
The challenge of a match we sat,
Win, lose or draw the bum was numb!

No word of wife or work was said,
Though some would, quietly, ring home,
Although they'd liked a lonely bed,
I never knew a one would roam.

The word 'relax' was never used,
We all had different work to do,
No one's complaints would be refused,
They never came from this 'mad' crew!

Roye, December 2003

Remembrance Day

Remembrance Day is here again, the medals polished
bright,
Parades are smaller year by year but still a stirring sight,
The Cenotaph, the Piper and the band that works so
hard,
The hymns that have been printed so that each may have
a card.

The bugle rings out, crisp and clear, its message to
convey,
So sharp across the years it sang, a very different day,
It told us that the time had come to do what had been
planned,
We thought the beach was clear and the causeways were
all manned,

But when we scraped up on the beach, everything had
changed,
They knew our target area and swiftly had us ranged,
For me it could have been much worse although it felt
like Hell,
Mortars and machine guns, a near miss from a shell.

161

Three times I hit the beaches and I saw them round me fall!
I, who gave so little, they who gave their all!

Roye, November 2003

The New Year

Another year has slipped away, there's one leaf left
again!
No snowdrops showing this time yet but crocuses are
through,
We've had no snow but lots of frost and lots of winter
rain,
The birds have stripped the berries and the cold turns
fingers blue.

The New Year's started cold and wet and has not been
too good,
The snowdrops haven't shown up yet but other bulbs are
fine,
The start we've had does not surprise; I never thought it
would,
We need a slightly offbeat start to age like good old
wine.

This year, I feel, is going to be the one I've waited for,
Some have been bad and some were worse but always in
my mind,
I knew that one would come along and level up the
score,
This one will be the best of all with the luck I always
find.

Roye, January 2004

Ghosts

I've seen many men die and some I have helped,
But don't think that's said as a boast,
I still feel the pain and I still feel the shock,
And I still know each separate ghost.

I don't think that I could have changed it.
I do know it's not what I'd chosen,
And I know that I'm full of remorse.

Some judge us not knowing the causes,
Though they've never had need to decide,
That to live there is no time for pauses,
You kill first or it's you that has died.

Roye, November 2003

The Cost

The war had more effect on me than I care to let be
known,
I've tried to hide it over many years,
The scars it left are hidden and never will be shown,
But nightmares re-awaken all the fears!

Some say they think I'm placid but it wasn't always so,
I'm not proud of many things that saved my life;
I've tried to be more tolerant and see what others know,
And remember I no longer NEED a knife!

It's hard to kill at distance till you know it's them or you,
It's infinitely harder right up close,
Your mind will tell you, later, all the things you should
not do,
But survival is the instinct that you chose!

Sometimes I think I've buried it so deep it can't return,
Until some unknown trigger brings it back,
And then I realize what was done you can't unlearn,
It's not possible to just wipe out your track!

I don't believe in God but I do believe in Fate and I
know that every one of us must go,
There's no evidence for one but the other is not needed
for no one lives forever as we know,
If you think that that's blind faith of the sort that fuels
God just look at what reality will show,
Fate is not a trick of words made by grasping little men,
it's a fact of life and always will be so!

Roye, 10th September 2004
(Anniversary of my Salerno Landing, 1943)

Wind in Autumn

The autumn breeze is rustling the tree-tops,
The sound it makes is pleasing to the ear:
The painter stops his brush strokes as he listens,
It indicates the closing of the year.
The leaves will soon be falling, now as always;
All yellows, browns and reds and even gold,
And brisk and ever colder are the short days,
The year still has its beauty though it's old.

Roye, September 2004

Stand Up Straight

Advice I got when I was young,
Sometimes I think the greatest,
Is when you're feeling really hurt,
That's when you stand up straightest.
Your foes will strike you when you're down,
And they'll be sure they've won,
That's when you'll throw the winning blow,
They know, too well, they're done!
You must not give them time to think,
Or time to strike once more,
The day is yours but you will know,
No pleasure in the score.
The instinct to survive is strong,
We all do what we must,
Sometimes though, it feels so wrong,
Even when it's just!

Roye, December 2004

Never Give In

When you reach four score and some,
And life's not feeling fun,
Take it by the scruff and shake it up!
It may treat you with disdain,
And be generous with pain,
Scorn it then and ask another cup.
Always drain it to the last,
For you can't relive the past,
Even if that's what you'd like to do!
What it's given you have taken,
Let's not show when we are shaken,
Just look around and enjoy all that's new.

I don't always feel that I'm eighty,
There are times when I feel Ninety Two!
But my years don't really feel weighty,
Since each day that I wake up is NEW.

Roye, January 2005

March 29th, 2005

We're married now for sixty years,
This Dunmore tale's not true,
We've had our share of family tears,
If you're honest so have you.

But what I have I would not change,
I know I never could,
Some people think they could arrange,
A life with all things good.

The truth is GOOD and BAD are there,
You can't decide the measure,
Just try and take a little care,
You know which you must treasure!

Roye March 2005

First Draft of "Still My Friend"

I think that I know what is coming
And I'm sure that it must be my turn,
I've no fear for whatever comes after
For only <u>believers</u> can burn!
It would hurt if I outlive my children
For both of them gave me some pause.
Now my Wife gives me frights much too often
For I know she has certainly cause.
It's not that I want to be leaving
I've certainly no wish to go
I wouldn't want anyone grieving
My life has been lucky I know.

My Friend has been good, true and caring
We've talked over years as I've said,
He will speak to me when he is coming,
When he does then I know I am dead!

Roye, March 2005.

You're Fine

Whenever you're asked you stand up straight and tell
everyone
You're fine,
Few need to know you're hurting bad and life isn't roses
and wine,
Only the closest can read the signs and know that you're
lying again,
You know that they know you're covering up and not
giving way to pain,
It's not always easy, in fact it is hard but do it without
too much noise,
And those who really do matter know that men have
been sorted from boys.

Roye, November 2005.

If

If you can keep your head when all about you are losing
theirs and blaming it on you,
If you can trust yourself when all men doubt you,
But make allowance for their doubting too,
If you can wait and not be tired by waiting,
Or being lied about, don't deal in lies,
Or being hated, don't give way to hating.
But don't look too good nor talk too wise:
If you can dream and not make dreams your master,
If you can think and not make thoughts your aim,
If you can meet both triumph and disaster.
And treat these two impostors just the same,
If you can bear to hear the truth you've spoken,
Twisted by knaves to make a trap for fools,
And watch the things you gave your life to, broken,
And stoop and build 'em up with worn out tools,
If you can make one heap of all your winnings,
And risk it on one turn of pitch and toss,
And lose and start again at your beginnings,
And never breathe a word about your loss;
If you can force your heart and nerve and sinew,
To save your turn, long after they are gone,
And so hold on when there is nothing in you,

Except the will which says to them; "Hold on!"
If you can talk with crowds and hold your virtue.
Or walk with Kings – nor lose the common touch,
If neither foes nor loving friends can hurt you.
If all men count with you but none too much,
If you can fill the unforgiving minute,
With sixty seconds worth of distance run,
Yours is the earth and everything that's in it,
And – WHICH IS MORE – you'll be a man, my son.

Rudyard Kipling